I lost my job 90 days ago. After I finished reading the first chapter of Employed by God, I found hope again.

—Brenda Wickard

What a moving story—and written in a way that is clear and compelling.

—Vinita Hampton Wright,

　　author of The Soul Tells a Story and Grace at Bender

　　Springs

In Employed by God, the reader will find courage, forgiveness, and spiritual growth.

—Pat W. Kirk,

　　Christians Read: Books Review

Employment and crisis are relevant topics for many in our congregation, and the study questions delve deeply into different issues that grew my faith.

—Lynn Copeland Buckles,

　　director of Christian Education at Tabernacle United

　　Methodist Church, VA.

This enticing memoir of faith discusses rising to God's call and is a much recommended pick for Christian studies collections.

—Michael Dunford,

　　Midwest Book Review

Employed by God

God

Benefits Packaged with Faith

BY

TRACY S. DEITZ

Employed by God: Benefits Packaged with Faith

Copyright © by Tracy S. Deitz

ISBN-13: 978-1466370821
ISBN-10: 1466370823

Library of Congress Control Number: 2011917642
CreateSpace, North Charleston, SC

Some names of real individuals have been changed or omitted to protect confidentiality. In all other cases, real names have been used with permission.

Scripture quotations are taken from the HOLY BIBLE, NEW INTERNATIONAL VERSION ®, *NIV* ®. Copyright © 1973, 1978, 1984 by the International Bible Society. Used by permission of Zondervan. All rights reserved.

Excerpt from CLOUT: TAPPING SPIRITUAL WISDOM TO BECOME A PERSON OF INFLUENCE, copyright © 2003 by Stephen R. Graves and Thomas G. Addington, reprinted by permission of John Wiley and Sons, Inc.

Excerpts from THE SUPERNATURAL WAYS OF ROYALTY, copyright © 2006 by Kris Vallotton and Bill Johnson, reprinted by permission of Destiny Image Publishers.

For all those who face broken dreams
and still have the courage to believe

Psalm 23

A PSALM OF DAVID

The Lord is my shepherd, I shall not be in want.
He makes me lie down in green pastures, he leads me beside quiet waters,
he restores my soul. He guides me in paths of righteousness for his name's sake.
Even though I walk through the valley of the shadow of death, I will fear no evil,
for you are with me; your rod and your staff, they comfort me.
You prepare a table before me in the presence of my enemies.
You anoint my head with oil; my cup overflows.
Surely goodness and love will follow me all the days of my life,
and I will dwell in the house of the Lord forever.

Contents

Acknowledgments

I'd like to express my gratitude to the following people:

My husband, Dan, who taught me to believe that with God, all things are possible.

My sons, who encouraged me to chase after my dreams.

First readers Elaine Rutherford, Clay Orsborne, Letha Jones, Robin Kelley, Mike Meara, Kelly Rucker, Jody Trenary, Damon Yaughn, Denise Swett, Alison Bareford, Shellie Sweeney, Marvin Fields, Jennifer Humphrey, Ray Liptrap, Margaret Rose, Bill Carmichael, Amy King, and Margaret Kackley, who believed the story had a message worthy to share and encouraged me to keep writing.

Members of the Spotsylvania Writers Club and the Riverside Writers (a chapter of the Virginia Writers Club, Inc.) for their support and painstaking help in revision after revision.

The James River Writers for an outstanding fall 2009 conference and instruction about the business of publication.

The Northern Virginia Writing Project for showing the power, and safety, in collaborative writing groups.

NaNoWriMo Web encouragements on how to quantify writing goals and get ideas down.

For participants, organizers, and faculty at the 2010 Mount Hermon Christian Writers Conference who honor God and teach how to emphasize his universal truths.

Editor Kathy Ide for polishing the manuscript like grandmother's silver.

Rev. Richard M. Carbaugh of Fredericksburg, who delivered a Good Friday message that revealed that God doesn't wait for us to meet him on the mountaintop, but instead he descends to join us in valleys.

Lynn Copeland Buckles, who came up with the title.

The Amazon CreateSpace team for help designing and producing the manuscript.

For all the other wonderful people in my family, church, and neighborhood who allowed me to share their lives and an intimate part of their spiritual quest searching for God.

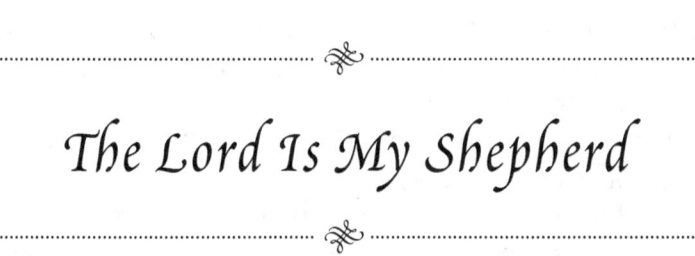

CHAPTER ONE

The Lord Is My Shepherd

I knew something was wrong the moment I saw my husband's chalky white face as he slipped into my basement cubicle. Although Dan and I were civilian employees in the same military organization, we worked in separate buildings. We rarely entered each other's work space. Dan had been fine two hours earlier when we drove to the office. What had happened to change his normally cheery countenance to one of foreboding?

He passed the two employees in front of me without speaking. Then he made eye contact with me, put his finger to his lips to signal silence, and motioned for me to follow. I logged off the computer and left the desk. My coworkers appeared oblivious to the unfolding drama.

Dan hurried down the gleaming metallic hall and ducked into a cluttered, seldom-used printer room. "Tracy, John just pulled me out of a meeting about Afghanistan so I could give you the news." He took a deep breath. "If you haven't resigned by ten a.m., they're going to terminate you. You have ten minutes to decide."

I felt like someone had kicked me in the stomach, but I was too proud to collapse. "Why? What did I do wrong?"

"I don't know. John wouldn't tell me."

I wasn't sure whether to start crying or cussing. To my credit, I did neither. I wanted to be brave, for him and me. "It's okay. I hate this job anyhow."

Although I didn't like the solitary computer work and felt miserable in the rigid security environment, I'd spent six months learning many new skills as an entry-level technical editor. I resented being branded a failure, particularly without the courtesy of conversation to review where my performance fell short.

"It's better if you resign," Dan said. "Won't look as bad on future job applications."

I longed for my husband to enfold me in a hug that reassured me everything was going to be all right. However, he had a job to do. I did, too—for about nine more minutes.

"Do you want me to stay?" he asked.

Dan was worried about me, which felt nice, but he needed to finish his urgent meeting. I couldn't ask him to step into my battle. God had seen me through worse; I would trust him now. "No, go ahead. I'll be okay."

He turned and rushed up the stairs.

Leaning against the wall of the tiny space, I collected myself mentally. I had never been fired. What did one do? I stared at the papers in the waste basket beside the printer. Like the trash, I was about to be thrown away with complete disregard. I might have understood if I'd done something wrong, but no guilty conscience plagued me.

The only recent change at work was that I'd asked John, the director of human resources, for help a week ago, hoping that he could help me find more collaborative writing assignments to balance out my computer work. Was *this* his answer?

Squaring my shoulders, I marched toward my desk. Movement dissipated some of the shock as I glanced at cubicles along the way. The area looked like a mausoleum, with people buried alive in individual crypts. Faint clicks on computer keyboards resembled fingernails scratching the inner lids of sealed coffins. I was about to be released from the company of the dead. My resurrection from a comatose career was unexpected, but not unwelcome.

I passed the two editors near my desk; neither appeared to have moved. How could they be so unaware of the cataclysm that had occurred?

I looked around my cubicle, considering where to start packing. My most precious possession was the orange-and-red sunset painting on the wall. My mom had brushed each daub of color, and her gift of time and self always calmed me. When I felt claustrophobic in the dark office space, I pretended the picture was a window. I took the artwork down and set it on the floor.

Then I cleared my locker, placing water bottles, aspirin, granola bars, and gym clothes into plastic bags. My Bible and daily devotional went on top of the pile. The passage that fateful morning of August 31 had been about joy. Being dismissed sure wasn't bringing happiness. How could God allow me to get fired?

Bags accumulated on the floor as I emptied the desktop. On the computer, I tagged page 43 of my current project so the supervisor would know the last section edited. I thought for a second about e-mailing the whole distribution list that I was being terminated for no good reason and extending condolences to all who remained in that stagnant place. Better judgment prevailed. After all, my husband still worked there. And now, he had to make the mortgage payment alone.

After logging off all three networks, I took a stack of papers to the shredder so that whoever had my desk next would find it clean.

Forty minutes had dragged by since Dan's warning. Ten a.m. had come and gone. Maybe I had misunderstood Dan. Was John expecting me to go upstairs to the personnel department?

Just as I reached for the phone to call and ask, John marched past the other editors and stopped at my cubicle. "I need to know your answer."

So much for second guessing. Or punctuality.

I stood. "I have some questions."

He turned his back and strutted down the hall. "Come with me to my office."

As I followed him, my fellow editors pretended like nothing was happening and wouldn't look at me.

In the other building, John positioned himself behind the desk. "What are you going to do?"

"First I want to find out what's happening. A week ago, you said you were going to talk with the chain of command about getting me some writing assignments."

"I did. They don't like people asking for a position they think fits them."

"They'd fire me for that?"

"You're a probationary employee. They can do whatever they want." He pretended to skim documents on his computer.

"Did anyone request my termination before I talked with you?"

"No." John averted his eyes.

"I want the opportunity to appeal."

"Then you'll have to be terminated first. If you leave on your own volition, you have no grounds to appeal."

But if I got fired, that went on my permanent record. And I had no guarantee that an appeal would have a positive outcome. Even if I won, the work environment would be miserable. I was trapped.

I glared at John. "Next time an employee asks for your help, you might mention that your assistance could result in being terminated."

He squirmed in his chair. Then he called in his assistant.

Betty escorted me to my cubicle. Her polite chitchat off-set the turmoil in my mind. When I picked up my bags of things to take to the car, she kindly offered to help. I handed her my peace lily.

"Is this plastic?" she asked.

"No, it's real. It's the only kind of plant I could find that would grow under the fluorescent lights."

Betty and I went to the car. "Your suit is lovely," she said.

"Thanks. Guess it was a good day to wear something cheery."

We left the parking lot to get the last load in the basement. "David," I said to the guy in the next cubicle, "you're losing your roomie."

He looked surprised and then sad. I don't know what he thought I'd been doing for the last forty minutes. He lowered his head and said nothing.

For the termination procedure, Betty led me to an anteroom outside the colonel's office. As the senior officer in my chain of command, he would conduct the hearing. She told me that she had to get paperwork from the HR office and would be right back.

As I sat in the metal chair, I thought, *Where is God in all this? Didn't he want me to stay here?*

My mentor, Jared, and I had prayed together on several occasions for wisdom about how to handle this job. Just one week before, in a quiet prayer time with God, I had specifically heard "Stay the course." That gave me the confidence to ask for John's help.

After ten minutes, Betty returned with a manila envelope and beckoned me inside the colonel's office. Camouflage-clad, the bald man bunkered behind his desk; two senior managers flanked him. Betty slid into a seat on my left, but John was nowhere to be seen. *How convenient for him.*

"Is this the hot seat?" I quipped. No one met my gaze.

"You are here to be terminated," the colonel said, his eyes cold and unyielding. He read my termination notice out loud, citing that I was a burden to the organization and hadn't acquired skills fast enough. He added that I didn't desire to excel in the position for which I'd been hired.

I wondered why none of the upper-level managers had asked me what was going on with these allegations.

Fear and confusion disappeared in a wave of indignation. "I was told that if I took the termination option, there would be an opportunity to talk about this."

"Sign the letter," the colonel said. He thrust the papers at me and pushed a pen across his desk, as though he feared contamination if our fingers touched.

All vestige of hope having disappeared, I signed the letter with a shaky hand. I squared my shoulders and held my head high as I left the room. *What jerks!*

As I left the building, anger with God resurfaced. Why hadn't he shown up to deliver me?

Or had he? During the first few months I'd been employed there, I had awakened each morning with joy at the thought of learning about other countries. But lately I'd been dreading the long days typing on a keyboard in silence.

On the drive home, I finally allowed myself to cry. Self pity, rage, and confusion vied for top seating. Why hadn't God protected me? What would happen now? I had more questions than answers. Prayer seemed a futile attempt to converse with someone who wasn't listening.

I Shall Not Be in Want

At 3:40 p.m., I sat in my kitchen, feeling alone and rejected. Of all the jobs I'd had over the years, I'd never left any without commendations for my work. I'd never even failed a class in all my years of school. I didn't know how to handle feeling deficient.

Desperately needing reassurance, I sent up a prayer: *Lord, I really need somebody to talk to. Could you please have someone call?*

Since he had said nothing during the crisis that morning, I steeled myself to endure more silence. Maybe God was mad at me for not trying harder to be a good editor.

But less than a minute after my prayer, the phone rang.

"Hey, Tracy, I was just thinking about you. What's going on?" asked my friend Shellie. She participated in a neighborhood Bible study held on Monday nights. Never before had she called me during working hours.

A sigh of relief rose from deep within my soul. God did hear after all. He cared. All hope was not lost.

Shellie and I talked for a few moments. She affirmed me and let me know I wasn't alone. More important than her words of assurance was the knowledge that God hadn't abandoned me. He wasn't working in the way I'd expected, but I had to trust that good would come of this.

Later that day, I called my twenty-one-year-old son to give him the news.

"Mom, be sure to focus on Dan and think about how he's feeling. He has to go back to work there tomorrow."

My son's concern about Dan's well-being humbled me because I was so wrapped up in my own pain that I hadn't considered how Dan might feel.

At the Bible study that night, my girlfriends consoled me. They didn't doubt me or indicate that I was a failure. They said that God would provide something better. Alison prayed that I would find my passion and purpose. Knowing they still believed in me touched my core.

The eventful day ended with Dan holding me. As he reached to turn out the light, he said, "We can go to sleep tonight knowing that we've done our best. I'm not sure others can do the same."

His loyalty comforted me.

The next morning, a friend from the neighborhood called. "The word for you today is that Jesus loves you," Rhonda said.

Her concern and thoughtfulness reassured me.

My dad also called to say he loved me. "You didn't like that job anyway. Leave it behind and move on. Dan will provide for you."

Dad's practicality removed some of the sting of failing.

"Don't be in a hurry to find something else. Take this time to reflect and determine what you really want to do."

His advice made sense, but I wasn't sure what I wanted to do. All day long, depression crouched over me. In spite of the kind words of my friends and loved ones, I still felt like a failure. Whispers of "worthless" hounded me.

The next day, just getting out of bed and showering were Olympic events. But I forced myself to take positive steps—no matter how tiny. I took a walk with Alison and soaked in a bubble bath. That was about all I got done, but it was a start.

I knew I had to start looking for a new job but wasn't sure where. After being a teacher for seven years, I had left the classroom to explore new challenges. That was when I took the editing job. I'd been pleased with myself for "advancing" from working with bright young minds to climbing the ladder of prestige and success. In that military basement, I'd had visions of glory and fame. God tempers pride in strange ways.

I e-mailed a middle-school principal that I'd like to volunteer helping at-risk students.

During the next week, every job application asked the dreaded question, "Have you ever resigned to avoid termination or have you been terminated?" How was I supposed to overcome that, particularly in a market with almost 10 percent unemployment?

I should have been able to let the loss go and believe God had something better for me, but my faith had taken a hit. Had God let me get fired as punishment? If so, where had I fallen short and disappointed him?

I wondered if Dan was embarrassed about me. We had been married only a year. Previously divorced from other long-term partnerships, Dan and I were both grateful to have a second chance. His adult daughters had accepted me fully and warmly. Would they now see me as incompetent?

I also worried about money. Dan and I had recently bought a house; our old one was still on the market. Could Dan manage two mortgage payments?

While I fretted, Dan encouraged me to trust God for justice and believe that things like this happened for a reason. I envied Dan's confidence in the middle of chaos. All I felt was panic.

Others also consoled me. Chris was a friend of Dan's I'd recently met. She came over to my house one quiet afternoon to visit. "You are pointed to a destination," she said as she and I sat on the screened porch, admiring the fall colors.

We read from Hebrews 11:1–2, "Now faith is being sure of what we hope for and certain of what we do not see. This is what the ancients were commended for."

Chris looked me in the eye. "God has said to you, 'Hey, Tracy, you didn't put on your big-girl pants and quit taking crumbs off the basement floor, so I plucked you out of there!'"

I laughed, but I heard the truth in her words.

Chris added, "God is also saying, 'Stop playing the why-did-I-get-fired game.'"

Her caring candor released me from guilt about losing the job. She shifted my focus from staring behind me to gazing ahead with confidence. How God would work through that termination was still a mystery, but I believed his grace would see me through until the next step became clear.

"It's amazing how directional our lives really are if we pay attention," Chris said.

Her quiet assurance gave me hope.

Verse 10 at the end of the Hebrews passage read, "Abraham was looking forward to the city with foundations, whose architect and builder is God." If I trusted him, he would construct something worthwhile and lasting. No part of my experience would be wasted. Even pain could be redefined into an asset.

During the next few weeks, I made peace with the waiting. The pain of rejection lessened, and I began to find joy again.

Outside activities restored a sense of balance. I got Dan's tire fixed and registered for painting classes. I also stopped at the library to check out books on positive thinking. At home, I read to discover new ideas and approaches for dealing with hardship. A passage from a book by Stephen R. Graves and Thomas G. Addington titled *Clout: Tapping Spiritual Wisdom to Become a Person of Influence* helped me to see a different perspective.

The best kind of clout emanates from moral strength, which generates security that we feel and that is visible to others—security and significance built not on titles, money, or achievement. Rather, our internal strength is built on spiritual identity and an understanding that we were created with a purpose by a master designer, and we can have an intimate relationship with that same God.[1]

I thought about this quote the next morning on the way to the local bakery for donuts. As soon as I entered the shop, the delicious smell of fresh-baked bread greeted me. The glass display showcased blueberry muffins, chocolate-slathered éclairs, and powdered-sugar confections. I chose two buttercream-filled donuts. Taking the donuts and milk outside, I sat in a café chair in the warm sun. With the first bite into the whipped cream, I thought that maybe termination wasn't awful after all. At eleven o'clock on a weekday morning, I was enjoying brilliant weather and sipping cold milk. Life was sweet.

As I absorbed these simple pleasures, my hair stylist, Daniela, walked up. "Hi," she said. "What are you doing?"

"I'm not working anymore, but this buttercream is making me realize that's not so bad."

"What happened?"

"I got fired. But I wasn't happy there anyway."

She smiled. "I understand."

I sensed no judgment on her part. Her matter-of-fact acceptance was another gift.

As she purchased her donuts, she cuddled her twenty-one-month-old son in her arm. The last time she had cut my hair, Daniela had told me part of her son's story.

---

1 Stephen R. Graves and Thomas G. Addington, Clout: Tapping Spiritual Wisdom to Become a Person of Influence (San Francisco: Jossey-Bass, 2003), 94.

When Gavin was born, he weighed one pound. He received round-the-clock nursing care, spending almost four months in neonatal intensive care. It was a miracle that he survived. He looked completely healthy now.

Even though my world seemed topsy-turvy, what I had suffered was nowhere near what others had endured and overcome. I wanted to be like Daniela and reveal peace and steadfastness, no matter the circumstances. The time for mourning had expired. All I had to do now was wait and watch for God's direction.

Over the next several months, as I did everything I could to find a new job, God provided numerous insights. Because I had more time on my hands than usual, he spoke to me more often and I heard his voice more clearly. Though often frustrated at the lack of response to my attempts to secure employment, as well as watching our savings dwindle and wondering how much longer we'd be able to pay our bills, I reveled in the deeper relationship I was developing with my heavenly Father.

In the following chapters, I share some insights gained during my struggle with unemployment. Some came out of reading certain books (another luxury I'd had little time for while employed full time); others were the result of the Lord bringing to my mind past experiences in which he had shown himself faithful, which helped me trust him more in my present trial. Some came as I lived through emotionally traumatic events that occurred after I lost my job.

Whatever testing you're going through right now, I pray that as you read about what the Lord said to me during this season, you will hear the Holy Spirit speak to your heart as well. Some of my experiences may remind you of something you've gone through in the past yourself, a time when God proved himself worthy of your trust. You may feel encouraged to read some of the books that helped me along the way.

Another resource you will find at the end of each section is a Bible verse that goes along with chapter headings.

There also will be questions for personal reflection or small-group study.

Ask God to speak to you as you travel this journey of faith alongside me. Then listen carefully for that still, small voice. He will direct you in the path he wants to you go, a path that he has laid out just for you, which will ultimately result in his honor and glory as well as your own joy and peace.

STUDY SCRIPTURE

I think of you through the watches of the night.
Because you are my help, I sing in the shadow of
your wings. My soul clings to you; your right
hand upholds me. (Psalm 63:6–8)

STUDY QUESTIONS

1. Night is the time when fears grow large and hope seems small. Describe a vigil you keep as your soul clings to God while you wait for dawn to arrive.

2. Share a time when you observed someone singing in the shadow of God's wings. How does that example empower you to face your difficulties?

3. Discuss the meaning of the phrase "your right hand upholds me." What ways has God supported you in a past crisis?

4. What area of your life do you need God's help restoring? Take time now to ask him for assistance and to hold you in the palm of his hand.

5. Imagine parking next to the passenger side of a luxury car outside a bank. As you look over, you see a huge rottweiler sitting in the passenger seat, staring back at you through its open window. Would you even think of reaching inside that vehicle? Of course not! That scene could be a metaphor for God: he is present, protecting us, even if we've stepped away for a moment.

CHAPTER TWO

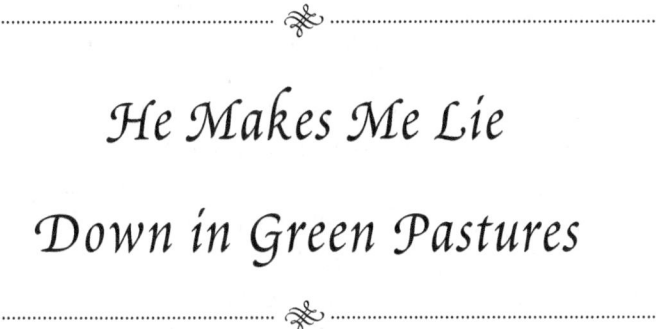

He Makes Me Lie

Down in Green Pastures

Weeks after being fired, I still had no employment, but two friends had recommended me for jobs at their respective offices. In one interview, the potential employer said I was overqualified, and I decided not to take that job. While I waited to hear about the other position, I maintained a confident spirit.

Meanwhile, my friend Alison had to place her elderly father in a nursing home because of his deepening dementia. He had been living in the home of his ex-wife, Alison's mom. The couple had been divorced for years, yet when he needed a place to stay, she generously vacated her one-bedroom townhome and stayed in the guest room of a girlfriend who lived nearby.

I felt sorrow at the decline of Alison's dad. He had been a charming host on several occasions when Alison and I had visited. I wanted to help her, and him, in any way possible.

One of Alison's brothers had agreed to stay with the father. But the son had been unable to provide the round-the-clock hospice care required by his father's failing medical condition. So, with great reluctance and guilt, the family found a nursing home for the dad.

Since I had plenty of time on my hands, I offered to accompany Alison the next time she visited him.

We entered a large, well-maintained plantation-style building. Wooden rocking chairs lined the arbor entry. White and red begonias graced the walkway.

Inside, a receptionist checked our identity cards and confirmed Alison's dad's room number. Stale air hovered in the tan hallway.

Alison and I passed a sun room with wicker chairs and windows overlooking gardens. We saw a fish tank with stately gray Oscars larger than a person's hand. In another sitting area, yellow-and-green Australian finches flew behind a glass panel. The tiny birds hopped back and forth from between wicker nests. These features made the facility a pleasant one.

Elderly patients, propelled by their own labored footsteps, inched past seated in wheelchairs. Most responded quickly to any overture of interest. A few faces were blank, the light from their souls hidden.

We found Alison's dad in his wheelchair in the hallway, looking around. A staff person approached him, pushing a cart with mushroom soup and crackers. Alison's dad requested chocolate fudge, which she gave him with a smile.

After we visited with him for a few moments, he asked to borrow Alison's cell phone to call an old friend and wish her a happy birthday. "Keyone was an exotic dancer," he said, winking at me.

He didn't ask for the phone, though, so I think he must have been teasing Alison. He lucidly asked about Alison's husband and sons.

"They're fine, Dad," Alison said.

Then he asked to borrow my camera to take pictures of property renovations for his clients. My heart ached at the way his mind went in and out of reality.

We wheeled him across the building to see the bird colony. Gouldian finches chirped and hopped about, rubbing beaks and tidying nests. Their flurry of activity contrasted greatly with the sedate pace of the elderly patients around them.

Alison took her dad out to the concrete patio to soak up the warm sunshine. He'd always loved the beach and had spent many years sunbathing in a chair by the ocean.

A middle-aged man and his elderly mom sat near us. He spoke to her in English, and she responded in her native tongue.

"Little grandmother," he said.

"Babushka," the mom chirped.

Their tender scene showed parenting in reverse: now the children taught the parents and took their elders for outings.

Alison called her sister in Florida and passed the phone to her dad so he could talk. That conversation went well, so Alison called her brother who lived out of state. But the dad got angry on the phone and wanted to know what the son was doing with the car left in his care.

Alison grabbed the phone, apologized to her brother, and promised to call him back. Then she glared at her dad. "Why did you do that?"

"He has all my stuff, and I want my car back."

"You know you aren't supposed to drive," Alison chided. "And I'm sure he's taking good care of your car."

"He never comes to see me."

"He lives in North Carolina, and his wife is expecting a baby soon. He can't come here all the time."

Once a fiercely independent wheeler-and-dealer, this man had become as fragile as the little birds flying near his wheelchair. He didn't have a wallet, car, cell phone—or his freedom. Although lovingly tended and secure, he still was confined.

I could relate to his vulnerability. I knew what it felt like to lose the ability to control the events of life.

When Alison announced that we had to leave, her dad tried to convince us to stay. Then he begged us to take him with us. When he finally accepted that we had to go without him, he asked Alison to push him outside the front entrance so he could see us leave.

As we neared the exit, he tried one last delaying tactic. "Tracy," he asked, "what's the breakfast cereal that makes a noise when you put it in milk?"

"You mean Sugar Smacks?"

He nodded and looked at his daughter with pleading eyes. "Would you take me to the grocery store so I can get that cereal for breakfast?"

Alison's face pinched in anguish. How could she deny him such a simple request? The nursing home provided all the patients' meals, and he was too frail to travel.

I couldn't stand to see her agony. I leaned down to look him in the eye. "Sir, we have to go now, but we'll be back soon."

He turned his head away.

Alison and I stepped toward the sliding glass door, but her dad wheeled closer, as though to follow. Alison turned around. "Dad, you can't go outside. If you try, they'll have to put a bracelet on you that sounds an alarm any time you get close to the door. Then you won't be able to go to the patio anymore."

He finally conceded to stay. Alison pushed his wheelchair back to his room. I waited at the entry, my heart breaking for both of them. I felt the same gut-wrenching emotion of when I left my son at kindergarten on the first day of school.

Alison's shoulders were slumped when she came back. As we exited the building, I wondered how to alleviate her pain. In the parking lot I hugged her and said, "You're doing all that you can to make sure he's safe. And this is one of the most beautiful and clean nursing homes I've ever seen."

She sighed deeply. No easy answers existed. Somehow, she would have to persevere and make the best of the situation. I knew how painful waiting and wondering were.

In life, we want lush green pastures in which to romp freely. But sometimes God puts us in enclosed locations designed for our well-being and protection. We have to trust him and find satisfaction in places where our needs—if not all our desires—are met.

Dear Lord, help me find contentment in this season of unemployment and accept your generous provision, without yearning ahead for more.

He Leads Me Beside Quiet Waters

Two weeks later, I went back to the nursing home with Alison. On the drive, she caught me up with what had been happening with her dad.

"I gave him a cell phone last week so he could contact his friends. I programmed numbers so he could call my mom or me with just the push of a button. But he's been making numerous 411 calls—at two dollars each—to get other phone numbers."

"Who's he been trying to call?"

"He phoned Hertz and told them to bring him a rental car. When they requested the address of the delivery, he asked someone on staff to provide the nursing home's address. They cancelled the order."

We shook our heads. Although I admired his spunk, safety issues were a big concern.

Even more than his security and health, Alison worried about her dad's spiritual condition. "I've tried talking to him about God several times. I told him not to be afraid of death. I reminded him of the time I was almost in a fatal car accident."

"You never told me about that. What happened?"

"It was several years ago. I was driving on the interstate, and my car got trapped between two semis. They dragged my car for a long, frightening moment. But then I saw a light and felt complete peace. Fortunately, one of the semi drivers saw my car and radioed the other one before I got completely crunched."

I quietly pondered the mystical transition from life to death. Even though no one knows exactly what will happen, we can find contentment in trusting that God has something more for us than the here-and-now. Being fired felt like a head-on collision, one that I had survived.

Alison said her dad had dodged every spiritual discussion she'd tried to have with him. He didn't deny having a saving faith, but he didn't confirm it either. She felt a vague sense of unease, but was unsure what else she could do.

"I found a copy of the twenty-third psalm in some of his papers the other day," she said, "so I read it to him."

I smiled. That passage had offered me tremendous comfort in my own times of need. Its reassurances also applied to me in this time of joblessness, fear, and doubt.

Sometimes, the hardest part of faith is trusting the direction in which the Lord leads. Being fired had dealt a death blow to my ambitions of career advancement. But God had accompanied me on every part of my life's journey so far. I believed that he could, and would, guide me to another place of fulfillment.

When we arrived at the nursing home, Alison went in first to make sure her dad felt like company. About fifteen minutes later, she came back to the front door, looking disturbed. "He's not so good today. You don't have to come in if you don't want to."

"I'm here to be with you. If it's okay with him, I'll go."

She nodded, and we walked back to his room. Her dad was in a fetal position on the bed, his eyes closed. His hair was uncombed. A skimpy beard of long, white whiskers hung from his chin. Swelling distorted his facial features, and his skin had yellowed.

I went to the bathroom to get a cool washcloth and found that the sink leaked. Two plastic bed pans below it overflowed with water. The faucet handles were missing. A few pieces of wet paper littered the tile.

Anger rose in me at such neglect. I left the room and asked a nurse about the leak. She said maintenance had a part on order, and they had no idea when it would arrive. In the meantime, he could use the bathroom down the hall.

Frustrated, I returned to Alison's dad's room. She had managed to get him to sit up, so I strode to the nursing coordinator's office.

"Hi," I said to the young woman. "I'm with the family in Room 121, and there's a problem with the sink. Could you please walk down with me and look at it?"

The coordinator followed me to the room. I pointed at the mess in the bathroom. "Someone could slip on the floor and fall."

The coordinator agreed to see what she could find out. After she left the room, Alison's dad ate a good lunch of chicken and rice, green peas, and chocolate mousse. He also took an anti-anxiety pill. An aide came to help him put on clean clothes so we could take him outside for sunshine and fresh air. With our company, the food, and the medication, he rallied.

The aide showed deep compassion and gentle care. She had wonderful rapport with Alison's dad. I reflected on how difficult her job must be, but she did it tenderly, without complaint.

The woman found a pair of clean sweat pants. Another nurse came to help put them on him. Alison and I stepped into the hallway to give them privacy.

Glass windows showed the cafeteria across the hall. A dozen elderly people milled around. A nurse spoon-fed a woman in a wheelchair. A patient who had one foot amputated used handrails to pull herself around the room in laps. A foursome hunched over a table, playing cards. In such limited circumstances, they seemed to make the most of their surroundings. Could I do the same without the structure of a paying job?

The aides left Alison's dad's room, carrying dirty linens. When we went back in, the room had a foul odor, and the bed was stripped bare. But Alison's dad sat in the wheelchair, looking alert.

We pushed him to the outside patio. The trip was slow. His wheelchair had no footrest, and he got tired of holding his feet up. He asked Alison to get him an Italian ice—pineapple.

He reached into his pants pocket and pulled out two crumpled one-dollar bills. "Tracy, will you get me some candy from the gift shop? They've got an order ready for me. I want to share it with you and Alison."

Touched by his thoughtful desire to offer hospitality, I took his money and headed for the small candy shop in the nursing home, allowing Alison and her father to have time alone together. When I found the shop, the sign on the door said Closed. No hours of operation were given. No indication of when the shopkeeper would return.

I passed the barber shop on the way back and thought Alison's dad might enjoy getting a haircut. Unfortunately, the door was locked.

The next place in the hall was the activity room. A television blared and puzzle pieces littered the table, but the room had no people.

Frustration welled within me. I'd failed at the simplest of missions. Alison's dad would be disappointed when I came back without candy.

When I returned to the patio, I saw Alison sitting next to her dad. Their shoulders touched slightly, and they faced the warming rays of the sun. Alison's dad napped peacefully.

I sat across from them and basked in their glow. Here, in a medical facility for people facing the end of life, the gifts of togetherness and acceptance were priceless. Alison displayed devotion for her dad—not in busyness, but being near. Could I slow my pace to enjoy such simple moments?

Alison's dad stirred when he heard us talking. I gave him back the crumpled dollar bills. He put the money in his pocket, not uttering the smallest complaint. The three of us sat in companionable silence and enjoyed the fall weather. Soon, Alison's dad drifted off to sleep again.

"We need to get him back," Alison said. "That medicine is really kicking in."

In the room, we found a maintenance guy working on the sink. A ladder stood in place of the bed, which had been moved to the middle of the room. Above, insulation peeked out from the ceiling near the water shut-off valve.

"Could you come back in about thirty minutes?" the worker asked.

Alison's dad had slumped farther down in the wheelchair. "I don't think so," I said. "He's practically falling out of the chair, and there's nowhere else for him to go."

Alison and I moved the bed a few inches away from the ladder. She asked an aide to help us get him out of the wheelchair.

When the aide saw the corner of a dollar bill poking out of his pocket, she cried out, "He's got money!" She peered at Alison.

My friend looked exhausted. "It's all right," I said. "It's only two dollars, and it's important to him."

Even though Alison's dad had an expense account at the nursing home, carrying those tangible bills empowered him. I didn't want to allow that small dignity to be taken from him.

Alison's dad curled up on the bed and went right back to sleep. The bedding had been stripped, and I didn't see any blankets. Alison looked in the closet and dug through the dirty laundry basket. She pulled out a fluffy blue fleece robe. "I guess this will do." She gently covered her dad with it.

The maintenance guy pointed to some faucet parts sitting on the bathroom counter. "I got these off another sink," he said, "We don't carry many in stock—too expensive. Sometimes I pay for stuff myself so we can get the job done."

Inwardly, I cringed at the implied low priority of the elderly stuck with malfunctioning equipment. "All the bathrooms are going to be remodeled soon. Supposed to be an eight-to-ten-million-dollar job."

As Alison made small talk with the maintenance guy, I thought about my own situation. I'd felt devastated because I lost a job. My pride was hurt, and I was concerned about financial commitments. However, only my ego had been damaged. That wasn't fatal.

An individual's net worth is far greater than any monetary value. So why did I measure myself by my ability to earn a paycheck? How much better to invest time storing up heavenly treasures.

Alison faced the loss of a beloved parent with courage and calm. She wasn't bitter or angry. She didn't rail against injustices. Sustained by God's quiet waters, she drank deeply to preserve an inner peace. She chose to live in the richness of each moment left with her dad, being grateful for what she had.

Her father may only have had a couple of bucks in his pocket, but his legacy of love for his children was vast. And he had been willing to give all the money he had to purchase a gift for the two of us.

Our heavenly Father's generosity also surpasses understanding. He renews beautiful nature for us throughout the seasons. He invests his companionship daily in our lives. He gave his Son to clear away all of our outstanding debts so that our accounts are paid in full.

STUDY SCRIPTURE

But store up for yourselves treasures in heaven, where moth and rust do not destroy, and where thieves do not break in and steal. For where your treasure is, there your heart will be also. (Matthew 6:20–21)

STUDY QUESTIONS

1. What are your most priceless possessions? Why are they valuable to you?

2. When the time comes for you to leave this earthly existence, what gifts do you want to leave behind for others?

3. Brainstorm ways you can support others who are facing bereavement. What specific behaviors would be least obtrusive and most appreciated?

4. In white-water rafting, riders zip along fierce currents. How does the thrill of this type of adventure contrast with resting beside quiet waters? Which scenario represents this stage of your life?

CHAPTER THREE

He Restores My Soul

After my visits with Alison's dad, I realized that the time
I had left to invest in God's kingdom was limited, and
I didn't want to waste a minute.

How did a forty-six-year-old who had been fired measure success? By reinventing a professional identity? Or by
rising above difficulty and believing God's goodness would
result? An opportunity to answer that question soon presented itself.

A couple whom Dan had known for years lived in
Columbus, Ohio. Tom and Beth invited us to be their guests
for an Ohio State football game during Halloween weekend. Dan and I eagerly accepted their invitation.

Tom picked us up at the airport. When I reached out to
shake his hand, I discovered he only had two fingers on his
right hand. He firmly covered mine with his left hand, too,
with no self-consciousness.

Losing my job had crippled me professionally, but that injury wasn't physical. Tom managed a more obvious loss with a graciousness that put everyone at ease.

While driving us to the Buckeye athletic complex, Tom shared his excitement about having recently joined the college staff after completing thirty-three years of coaching high school sports. I admired his ability to sustain a long-term commitment to service and transition to another level of performance when most people decided to retire.

Once on campus, he led us into an imposing room, three stories high, with towering metal-framed windows. Glass cases housed numerous trophies. From 1951 to 1978, Coach Woody Hayes led the Buckeyes to win five national championships. During Hayes's career, he had a 238-72-10 record and 205-61-10 in the Big Ten."[2]

"He put Ohio State on the map," Tom said.

And yet, Hayes had been fired for losing his temper at a game and striking players. Hayes' lack of self control destroyed his career. How had the famous coach handled that? I also wondered if Dan had told his friends that I'd recently been terminated. What character flaws did I have that contributed to my job loss?

"You're only as good as your last game," Tom said.

Inwardly, I winced. In that case, my record was poor.

Despite years of coaching successes, Hayes didn't rebound after the Gator Bowl fiasco in 1978. I had a similar obstacle to overcome in being fired. How could I earn the right to contribute somewhere else and repair my professional reputation?

Walking down the 120-yard hallway, we looked at team memorabilia, interspersed with phrases that identified spiritual and moral development as the top priority.

The team's tradition also emphasized community service. "There are eighty-eight elementary schools in the

---

2 "Coach Hayes." Ohio State University History, http://bucknuts. com/osuhistory/coachhayes.htm. Last accessed 25 June 2010.

city," Tom said. "And every second grader is read to by a Buckeye."

Despite demanding schedules, the players made time to serve. Now that I had lots of freedom, where could I help?

Tom pointed to marble Lombardi awards. "It's fitting the trophy is made of rock, to show the discipline required to win."

I didn't feel like marble. I felt more like Bubble Wrap, popping as soon as pressure was applied. My tough exterior camouflaged a fragile heart. Somehow, during my years of employment, I had gotten off track, thinking that success was calibrated by external things rather than what was in my soul.

Tom showed us the day's schedule for the team. "Players and staff report to the complex promptly at 7:33 a.m., not seven thirty. That way we remember exactly what time we're expected to be ready." The tight agenda nuanced attention to excellence.

Timing was everything—in sports and life. I wanted success right away, but what if my present failure was training for a more important victory later in the season? Waiting on God to reveal his direction was hard discipline.

Just past Archie Griffin's sixty-pound Heisman trophy was a four-foot-long red digital clock, counting down to the next great rivalry. The time showed in days, hours, minutes, and seconds. This tool heightened the awareness of every player as he passed the wall. Time was precious; every moment should be utilized to prepare, mentally and physically.

Next we looked at photos of former Buckeye leaders. "Since 1951, only one coach on that wall *wasn't* fired," Tom said.

A person who lived solely for the acclaim of man was bound to be disappointed. So often, we humans look at outward appearances to select our leaders. The glitzier, the better. God focuses on what's inside our hearts.

Having been benched from a "starter" position, I sulked. My anger at God began because my will had been crossed.

I wanted to be a superstar editor. My outlook centered on me. Without a snazzy job title and a paycheck, who was I?

My spiritual attitude turned ugly when I was relegated to obscurity. I acted like God was my agent, and I could dictate contract terms. I need to realize that whether anyone else noticed or commended my efforts, God knew.

At the end of the hallway, an old black chalkboard filled an inconspicuous corner. This simple exhibit had a plastic shield protecting writing in chalk.

"What's that?" I asked.

"That was found in the armory a few years ago," Tom said. "The notes are bullet points for a book that Woody Hayes started writing after he got fired."

I noticed the word *clutched* written in small, cramped writing. Next to it were cryptic phrases about Stalin and Hitler.

"Hayes was connecting events in World War II where leaders choked," Tom said.

Would I also "choke" and withdraw from future challenges because I feared more failure?

Another category was "Things Better Not Said." I laughed inside. Hayes and I had a lot in common.

"Funny Bounces" titled Hayes's twenty-second item. I asked Tom to explain that one.

"A football's not round, so it never goes where you expect it to."

That was life. Expectations and goals bumped along unexpected twists.

In the coaches' conference room a sign said, "Players live up to what you expect of them."

God's love wasn't conditional. He desired the best for me, as did my family and friends. I knew they were in my corner cheering me on to overcome this setback. I didn't want to disappoint them and had to figure out the next step.

One play Hayes made famous was called "three yards and a cloud of dust." Rather than rely on spectacular moves, Hayes advocated tenacious runs up the middle in the heat of battle.

I prayed silently, *God, you are my coach. I invite you to call the plays. I promise to give my best and keep running up the middle, even if no one else sees the struggle but you.*

That prayer got tested the next day. In cold, rainy weather, the Buckeyes played a shut-out game. I was the only person in the crowd of 100,000 who didn't enjoy it—other than New Mexico fans. Enraptured with the football game, Dan barely noticed I existed. Neither an epileptic seizure nor an alien attack could have drawn his eyes away from the field.

I hadn't anticipated feeling abandoned on the one vacation we'd taken in months. Battling a sense of worthlessness, I needed Dan's affirmation now more than ever. I withdrew into myself and entertained discouragement.

The impasse lasted through Saturday night and into Sunday morning, when Tom and Beth drove us to the airport. Dan and I needed to work through the conflict; however, I wasn't going to break the ice. My lips stayed zipped as tightly as the luggage.

Dan must have liked the quiet, because he flipped through magazines in the airport unperturbed while I watched passengers.

A young mother waited at the terminal gate with us. She traveled with two daughters: one an infant, the other three years old. The mom tucked the fussy, fuzzy-headed baby under a throw blanket to nurse. Not wanting the three-year-old to get bored or feel left out, she invited her older child to sit on her crossed legs. She gave the toddler a makeshift pony ride while continuing to nurse the baby.

I admired how that mom used imagination, and what she had, to comfort her children.

God multitasks even more easily than that. Yet I'd limited him to one or two options. His perspective was broader. He allows difficulties to develop us, strengthen us, and teach us to rely on him. His love is pure. He felt my pain and was already moving to meet my needs, even if I doubted his help.

I wanted to ask Dan to forgive me for acting rotten, but I didn't. Stubbornly silent, I waited for him to take the initiative. I glanced sideways; he was engrossed in an article.

Looking around the terminal, I saw a female security guard approach a Catholic nun seated nearby. The nun wore a brown habit with a black wimple and a starched white neck covering. A long rosary hung at her side.

The guard leaned toward the nun and said, "Sister, the security officer found this by check-in and thought it might be yours." She held out her palm, which held a tiny gold crucifix on a broken piece of delicate chain.

The nun stroked the icon with reverent fingertips. Then she shook her head and withdrew her hand.

My chain of faith had been broken by disappointments. I had lost my belief that I mattered to God and that he had called me to a significant role in life. I'd been fired and my husband was bored with me; how could God love me? Did his heart really beat for me with a passion as high as the heavens? I longed to crawl into God's forgiving embrace, as well as Dan's.

Boarding began for our flight. As Dan and I moved toward the gate, the attendant informed the woman behind me, "Ma'am, you have three bags. Please consolidate them to two before you proceed down the jetport."

Glancing back, I saw the traveler rearrange her belongings until she had one heavy bag on her shoulder that caused her to list like a sailor on high seas. Behind her, she dragged a bulging carry-on suitcase.

Not even her elephantine handbag could have contained the negativity I lugged around. I was going home to emptiness. My spiritual self felt void.

Black silhouettes of travelers moving in front of the glass walls of the terminal reminded me of shadows following me. They represented getting fired, nearing middle-age, and feeling useless.

The huge dark eye of the control tower viewed the runway from column legs of concrete. The eerie, remote fixture made me wonder if God was staring down at me.

Once all the passengers settled into their seats, the plane inched forward in a line on the tarmac. The tails of the planes looked like dorsal fins of sharks, circling me with ravenous doubts.

Stenciled under the pilot's door of a Jet Blue plane was the phrase "Peek a Blue."

I often played peek-a-boo with God. But when my hands covered my eyes, that didn't mean God wasn't present. His reassuring grin prevailed every time I slid my fingers down to hazard a look.

"Ladies and gentlemen, we are ready for departure," the captain said. "Flight attendants, please be seated."

Wouldn't it be nice if God gave such precise directions? Then I would know at all times what to expect.

Cold air blasted from the vent above as the motors revved. The white stripes on the runway blurred. Wheels lifted from the ground. As the plane climbed, the scenery outside my window changed. What had seemed large before appeared miniature. I hoped the same would be true for my problems.

A few seconds into the ascent, the engines cut back drastically. The wing on my side dipped ninety degrees, and my stomach lurched. A woman behind me gasped. My heart rate tripled; my body tensed. I held my breath for several long seconds until the plane righted.

Then I saw the reason for the erratic pattern. As our plane crested the cloud cover, another aircraft emerged from the gray mass right below. Flight control had steered us safely away from a midair collision.

God would do the same for me if I let him. As a human, my vision and capability are limited. Tense moments of God's redirection need not terrify me. The adjustment will ensure my safe arrival. God sees the big picture and will always guide.

My heavenly Father delights in providing for me. I shouldn't be dependent on Dan, or a job, for my identity. God fashioned the universe with such care and attention that he knows whenever a sparrow falls to the ground. So why do I only approach him when I'm desperate? Isn't it God's pleasure to interact with his children and give them good gifts?

From an elevation of ten thousand feet, the sky looked like crystal, and the expanse seemed limitless. "As the heavens are higher than the earth, so are my ways higher than your ways and my thoughts than your thoughts" (Isaiah 55:9–12).

When Dan and I left Columbus, I saw only an overcast sky. But the view from a higher altitude revealed more. The layer of forbidding gray clouds gave way to a top sheet resembling polar ice. Covering that was a teal strip decorated with bouquets of wispy white clouds. Higher yet, a deep blue expanse stretched from the horizon to forever.

God challenged me to hold his hand as I traveled. Whether the times ahead had joy or sorrow, he wanted to stand beside me. In the times I felt most alone, he would be closest if I took my hands off my eyes and met his loving gaze.

He spoke to my heart during that flight. *These airplanes need time to rest, refuel, and be cleaned before they can go on again. You, too, need time to prepare and gain speed to sustain flight.*

God's words disconcerted me, but also reassured me.

When I was a young person, the teachings in the mainline conservative church I attended didn't indicate that God liked personal connections. He was represented mostly as that great other, whom I'd meet in heaven one day.

As I grew older, I reconciled Sunday school stories with what the world taught. If I conceded that God was powerful enough to create skies and ocean depths, then surely an intimate conversation wouldn't be beyond him. After all, science had already proven the existence of invisible sound and light waves. Maybe God chose his own broadcasting station for those willing to listen.

In my youth, I thought about God speaking only with words like "Thus sayeth the Lord," followed by the strike of a lightning bolt. But as an adult I learned that God preferred plain conversation, even when thunder may have been more effective.

Sometimes, instead of listening, I clapped hands over my ears and muttered, "Lalalalalalalala," because I didn't want to hear his guidance. Other times, my barrage of complaints blocked any direction God might offer.

Halfway to Charlotte, I decided I was tired of giving Dan the silent treatment. "Why aren't you talking to me?" I asked.

He looked up from his magazine. "I've been catching up on my reading."

"That makes me feel ignored."

"You want a magazine too?" Dan smiled.

I alternated between rage and respect for him.

He put up his hand for a high five, requesting my acknowledgement of his triumphant good line. I gave him one. The ice now broken, we began the work of resolving our conflict.

Marital intimacy requires honesty, respect, and a commitment of time. These qualities apply to our relationship with God too. Although he is the supreme being, he desires our company.

STUDY SCRIPTURE

For great is your love, higher than the heavens;
your faithfulness reaches to the skies. Be exalted,
O God, above the heavens, and let your glory be
over all the earth. (Psalm 108:4–5)

STUDY QUESTIONS

1. What part of nature reminds you most of God's glory?

2. How does God speak with you? What personal insights has he recently communicated?

3. Discuss with someone an example of when science seemed to clash with religious teachings. How did you resolve the conflict in your own mind?

4. What helps restore your soul?

CHAPTER FOUR

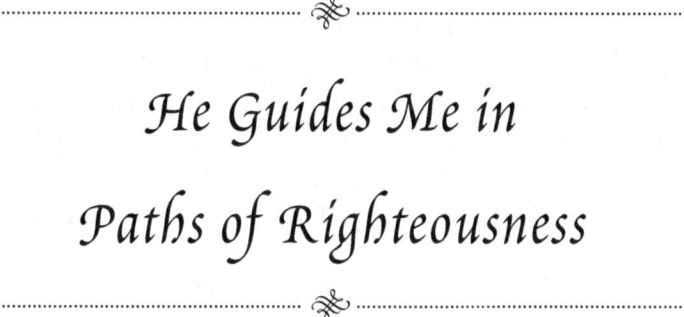

He Guides Me in

Paths of Righteousness

Many of God's opportunities come disguised. While we look for gifts in pretty boxes with neatly tied bows, the presents from God often arrive in seemingly unattractive packages. Before being fired, I thought getting a pay raise and promotion measured progress and God's favor. In this season, God provided a husband who was happy with me being a homemaker. God also surprised me by sending encouragement through a former neighbor.

"Tracy," Lundy said over the phone, "A job is opening at the education department of the hospital where I work. You'd be perfect for it. Send me a copy of your resume. I'm going to hand-deliver it to the lady in charge of hiring."

"Wow! That is exciting," I said. "Thank you so much for thinking of me."

"Be sure to fill out the online application too," Lundy said. "I'll keep in touch."

Meanwhile, time off from a rigorous work schedule allowed me to follow up with medical care since lab results indicated that I might have cervical cancer. While doctors tended my body, the Lord sent chances to interact with friends to heal my feelings of rejection. I also sought comfort from biblical examples of people who endured difficulty and had breakthroughs.

In the Old Testament, the Israelites sought deliverance from their enemies, the Philistines. Most Israelites saw only the gigantic Philistine leader, Goliath, who taunted them daily. However, youthful David perceived potential for victory. While grown men cowered, David placed his confidence in God. "Let no one lose heart on account of this Philistine; your servant will go and fight him," David told Saul in 1 Samuel 17:32.

I found David's words encouraging, and I couldn't wait to share them with my evening Bible study group with Elaine, Shellie, and Alison.

After exchanging our insights on this passage, Shellie said, "I think it's helpful to name our giants." We all agreed to take turns identifying the obstacles in our lives.

"Aloneness," Alison said.

"Mine is rejection," I added.

Shellie laughed. "I have a whole family of giants! Doubt, fear, and worry are at the top of my list."

"Me too," said Elaine.

We read more of 1 Samuel to see what God had to say about overcoming. When David's king expressed doubt, David boldly declared, "The Lord who delivered me from the paw of the lion and the paw of the bear will deliver me from the hand of this Philistine" (1 Samuel 17:37).

David had a history with God. When no one was watching—while David was alone in the fields guarding the sheep—God protected him from certain death. When David faced a lion, God didn't intervene with a hurricane to sweep the threat away; he gave David strength to over-power the creature. When David came across a bear, God could have chosen to swallow the beast in an earthquake. But he didn't. God equipped David to meet and defeat the dangers in his life.

God does the same for us today. He rejoices in the ordi-nary man or woman, boy or girl, who believes in an extraor-dinary God and charges into the lair of the enemy, fully equipped with spiritual armor for the battle.

Giants don't like brave foes. Their forte is to bully and scare with awful-sounding threats. "Am I a dog that you come at me with sticks?" Goliath challenged David. "Come here, and I'll give your flesh to the birds of the air and the beasts of the field!" (1 Samuel 17:43).

At that moment, David had serious decisions to make. Hesitation would sentence him to almost certain death, because the giant steadily approached. Running offered little hope, as the giant held multiple weapons.

"You come against me with sword and spear and jave-lin," David said, "but I come against you in the name of the Lord Almighty, the God of the armies of Israel, whom you have defied. This day the Lord will hand you over to me, and I'll strike you down and cut off your head" (1 Samuel 17:45–46).

No uncertainty quavered in David's response. Cutting off someone's head was a pretty definite outcome. David's absolute belief in the trustworthiness of God had been built over time in a variety of circumstances.

How could I get to that same place of confidence?

I thought about this the next morning while preparing to help a friend drive to North Carolina. She too struggled to find her way in a life filled with unknowns. Tammy faced a battalion of giants, one of which was a life-threatening ill-ness due to adrenal-gland failure. "One out of a hundred thousand people contract this illness," she told me.

In addition to her poor health, Tammy had two preteen children, Robert and Connie, whom Tammy and her husband had adopted years ago from overseas orphanages, as well as a seventeen-year-old son, Arnold, who had problems with authority figures. Arnold's antagonism with his stepfather, Tammy's husband, had taxed the marriage and led Tammy to send her son to North Carolina to stay with friends.

A falling out between Arnold and Tammy's husband had resulted in the necessity for a court appearance. Tammy asked if I could help with the driving on her three-hour trip to North Carolina to pick up Arnold. Since I had no job, I was free to accompany her and, hopefully, provide moral support.

We met at a grocery store parking lot halfway between our homes. Concerned about how her medical condition might affect her on this trip, I asked, "How are you feeling?"

"A little weak," Tammy said.

"Would you like me to drive first?"

"Please."

I walked to the driver's side and got in the blue van. In the back seat sat the two younger children. Tammy settled into the front passenger seat.

We passed the first leg of the trip in pleasant chitchat, which held at bay the questions tormenting Tammy about what would happen when she picked up her older son.

Tammy wore a brave face, but I knew from previous conversations that she was losing hope that she could meet all the demands placed on her. Giants loomed over her, threatening to conquer.

We made a pit stop at a 7-11. Robert rushed inside ahead of me. "Hey," I teasingly chided, "how about holding the door for me?"

He looked surprised, but he stepped back and waited for me to enter.

Inside, Connie created a slushy, alternating sections of blue raspberry with red cherry. The rest of us got other snacks.

On the way back to the car, Robert not only opened the store door for me, but also the car door. That kid was a quick study.

The second half of the trip passed quietly. Connie fell asleep. Robert seemed to disappear into the world of his headsets.

We rode in silence past the North Carolina state line over back roads and around marshy plots of land. "We can stop at this small diner for lunch," Tammy said. "It's a dive, but the hamburgers are good and it's only a few blocks from where Arnold's staying."

We parked in the dirt lot by the one-story block building. As we entered, an avalanche of cigarette smoke hit me.

I told Tammy what I wanted to eat, then said, "I'm getting sick to my stomach from all the smoke in here. I've got to go outside."

Tammy placed the order for all of us, settled the kids on stools at a counter near the cook, then joined me in the parking lot.

Safe from overhearing ears, Tammy started unloading the fears consuming her. "I hate my marriage. I want to die. I can't see any way out except death."

I stared at this beautiful woman in her thirties, who had two of the sweetest, coolest kids I'd met in a long time. Her blue eyes were filled with despair.

"I don't have any reason for living," she said.

I peeked through the window of the restaurant, where the kids were being entertained by an elderly lady shoveling frozen patties on the large grill. "I can see two good reasons right now." My heart broke for her, but speaking the truth in love was more important than pampering her feelings.

"They're already better off, even if I'm not here," Tammy said. "At least they're out of the orphanage."

I wanted to pop her. "How could you think they'd be better off without you? You are the sparkle in their lives. You bring them creativity, joy, laughter. Stop talking about death."

Tammy's chin dropped at my candid remarks.

"I know the Bible says God hates divorce," I said. "But there's got to be something between living with a broken marriage and death."

"You don't understand what it's like for me. I can't keep going on like this with things never getting better."

"God has seen me through many tough times, and he will help you too. He provides in unexpected ways. Remember how you stood with me when I was getting divorced?"

She nodded.

"I prayed for a lot of years that my first marriage would heal, but it didn't. Somehow, God helped me get through all the heartache."

A flicker of hope sparked in Tammy's eyes. Before she could speak, Connie bounced out the front door. "We need a five and some change."

While Tammy dug through her purse, I realized that this innocent child had just described what her mom desired: having five minutes to herself without the pressures of family and seeing change that indicated healthy growth in a relationship.

Tammy took the money inside, then came out again with the children, carrying paper bags of sandwiches. We all got in the car and headed out.

Although the hamburgers smelled good, I no longer had much appetite. I didn't know if my queasy stomach was a result of the smoke or from hearing that Tammy wanted to give up on life. How could I encourage her to hold on to hope and trust God to defeat her giants?

We drove deeper into the country, along marshy fields that stretched for miles. I contrasted this farming hamlet with the suburban neighborhoods we'd left in the morning. It was almost like we'd traveled back fifty years in a time machine.

Tammy turned onto a sandy lane leading to a run-down wooden house, the home of Tammy's friends who'd taken in her older son.

We walked up wooden porch stairs marked by chipped paint. At the top, a plastic bag full of garbage sat beside a damp mop. The door was wide open, so Tammy hollered "Hello" and walked inside.

When we entered the room, Tammy introduced me to Arnold. He had his mother's curly golden locks and Roman nose. His green T-shirt didn't quite cover his stout midriff, and pajama bottoms with a beer logo hung low on his hips.

We got out the hamburgers and ate in uncomfortable silence. Then we helped Arnold load his few possessions into the van. Sorrow permeated the air as he said good-bye to the friends who had given him a haven in the midst of his crisis.

As Tammy drove across the marsh, I tried to engage Arnold in conversation. "Did you go fishing out there?" I asked, nodding at the wetlands surrounding us.

"No. Too many copperheads. We saw a four-foot one sailin' across the water once. I shot its head off."

The issues facing this young man were more poisonous than any snake.

He must have been frightened, but he didn't let on. Instead, he donned earphones and jacked the sound up loud enough that I could hear his music in the front seat. It almost drowned out the car radio, which played a song rejoicing about being alive.

I hoped Tammy's heart strings were listening to the lyrics. She had all of her children with her. Together, with God, they could face whatever might come.

Since the day had been long, and the other two kids had ridden for hours, we detoured for a short walk along Virginia Beach before heading home. As soon as we parked, Arnold took his skateboard and headed toward a tourist shop. He said nothing to his mom.

"Meet us back at the car in ten minutes," Tammy yelled at him.

The younger kids, Tammy, and I strolled to the boardwalk. They took off their shoes and wiggled toes in the cold sand.

The salt breeze washed away the stale cigarette smoke still clinging to our clothes from the rustic diner.

Robert, Connie, and Tammy posed by the waves for a picture. Would this be their last family portrait? I shook the morbid thought out of my head.

The children roamed along the shore, picking up pieces of shells and gull feathers. They soaked up the healing peacefulness of the ocean's lullaby. I was glad we'd stopped. At least those kids would have one memory of joy from this difficult day.

During the entire trip, neither Robert nor Connie had uttered a single complaint or demand. They never once exhibited a bad attitude. Instead they graciously came alongside to help and gratefully accepted any gifts offered. Those young people faced adversity and uncertainty, yet they showed a calm beyond their circumstances.

Arnold and Tammy were also wounded. They suffered many hidden hurts.

I wanted to protect them all. Though guilty of many mistakes myself, I knew God still loved me. "For all have sinned and fallen short of the glory of God, and are justified freely by his grace through the redemption that came by Christ Jesus" (Romans 3:23–24). How could I convey that tender acceptance to Tammy and her family? Only God could show her the right path to take.

Connie scooped up a handful of sea foam and ran to her mother to show off the treasure. Tammy leaned forward to examine Connie's find. She zoomed her camera lens on the intricate, delicate bubbles.

Life was that fragile and temporary. I prayed for eyes to see such priceless gifts.

"Take a picture of me," Connie sang out. "I'm standing on top of a mountain."

In actuality, she was on a large mound of white and gray sand. However, that moment symbolized the courage of someone who climbed above circumstances and stood tall.

We joined Arnold at the van and began the long drive back to Spotsylvania County. Everyone seemed relaxed. Tammy turned up the radio. The country singer's voice crooned about how just being able to breathe is a blessing.

I knew Tammy's heart held more love than fear, even though the giants would try to tell her otherwise. I felt God specifically orchestrated that radio song to encourage her.

For the next hour, Tammy drove while the rest of us napped. After a gas stop thirty minutes from home, I took the wheel. Tammy curled up in the passenger seat beside me, appearing exhausted. Within moments, Arnold practically exploded with the concerns that had been eating at him.

"Why do I always have to be the one to leave? I take it and take it. Then when I stick up for myself, I get in trouble." Arnold crossed his arms and slumped in his seat. "I hate humanity. All people do is lie and take advantage of others."

I understood how he felt, but I encouraged him to realize that we all had choices. Even if others made unkind decisions, he didn't have to.

"What chance do I have?" he said. "I've been in and out of institutions my whole life. I don't even have a decent education."

"You can you read, can't you?" I asked.

"Yeah."

"Then you can get an education. You just have to find out information for yourself." I felt compassion for him, but condoning a sense of victimization would have crippled him.

Tammy had been following our conversation, but she remained quiet.

"I don't know math," he grumbled.

"I used to teach high school. I can help you, if you want."

He paused, considering the offer. Then he muttered, "The only way I can make money is if I sell drugs."

"Then you'll be part of the very humanity you despise," I said.

He frowned in thought.

"Look, you're bright and articulate. You've got a lot to offer. If you don't like where you are now, do something different."

"That's right, Arnold," Tammy said. "You used to have a good job at McDonald's."

"Arnold, maybe you could talk to your old manager. If you got that job back, you could save some money. That way you can get your own place so you don't have to worry about leaving again." I couldn't let Arnold convince himself that quitting was the only option. I wanted to say something that sparked hope.

Arnold looked at Robert and Connie in the back with him. "At least they've got *two* parents who love them. I've only got one."

Blinded by his own pain, Arnold didn't consider how his outburst might affect the younger children. They sat quietly with blank faces, but I knew they heard every word. I felt like swatting Arnold on the head. I wondered if he would ever be healed from the self-absorption that wounded those around him.

"Do you think this is a piece of cake for them? Their family is falling apart," I said. "But they've ridden in this car all day to pick you up and haven't complained once."

Arnold dropped his head.

"You know, I used to teach at a prison for young men. Many of them didn't even have one parent who loved them."

All the anger and bluster left him. I now saw the frightened face of a young man who faced many of his own giants: rejection, hopelessness, impossibility, poverty.

"Life used to be a simple straight line," Arnold said softly. "But now it's a bunch of squiggly mazes."

"That's brilliant," I said. "You have a sharp mind. You're going to figure this out."

"Arnold, I know you can do it," Tammy added.

When Tammy dropped me off, I hugged her, infusing her with as much tangible love as possible. I told the children the trip with them had been pleasurable. I assured Arnold that I'd be praying for him. As I drove home, I thanked God for my availability to take this trip with my friend and her kids. I hoped I'd made a difference.

Sometimes, life's issues tangle us up. Only God can give us true relief. His Word steers us to the right choices. He has a plan for us all. As we encourage one another and seek his direction, we can get a little further out of the entanglement of our fears.

STUDY SCRIPTURE

Be joyful in hope, patient in affliction,
faithful in prayer. (Romans 12:12)

STUDY QUESTIONS

1. When have you come alongside someone who courted despair? How did you encourage that person to rediscover hope?

2. Share a time when you felt nudged by God to speak the truth in love. What aspects of candor make healthy confrontation successful?

3. Describe a time when someone's caring insight changed the course of your life.

4. Have you ever seen someone be "right" but not "righteous"? How would you explain the difference?

CHAPTER FIVE

For His Name's Sake

In addition to spending time helping friends, I also sought educational opportunities. One of these included attending a one-day women's leadership conference at the local university. I hoped I could network there and find job leads. I had heard nothing about the hospital position in several weeks, but Lundy e-mailed that she would follow up for me so I still was hopeful.

At the leadership conference, I sat at a table with several other women. As a get-acquainted exercise, we shared dreams of things yet unrealized. One woman said she wanted to trade her career for having children. I explained about being fired and hoping to write a book that would encourage others.

Bunny, who manages a homeless shelter that serves five counties, sat across from me. She listened intently to my story and said that many people in circumstances similar to mine recently had sought refuge in her facility, the Thurman Brisben Center.

I wondered how long Dan and I could manage on one income. I feared bills would pile up and that would put too much pressure on Dan. So far, he had been patient and encouraged me to enjoy the time off. Although his earnings provided for our necessities, we couldn't absorb many unexpected expenses. What happened when people lost jobs and couldn't make rent or mortgage payments?

I looked at Bunny and asked, "Would it be okay if I visited you to learn how others are handling the setback and write about that in an article?"

"Sure," Bunny said. "We can set an appointment for next week."

Her willingness to help surprised and delighted me. Bunny's hospitality demonstrated faith in action that I had been reading about in my quiet time from a book by Carolyn Custis James titled *The Gospel of Ruth*.

In this book, Mrs. James reflected that each of us has the power to bless the lives of others when we take action personally to bring the love of Jesus into their lives.[3]

I appreciated Bunny's offer and looked forward to visiting the center, which had been started by area churches. Her serious consideration of me as a writer also bolstered my self-esteem. I fervently prayed that my husband and I would not end up needing to utilize the center's services someday.

On the day of the appointment, I climbed into my husband's 1978 truck because my car was in the shop for repairs. The truck looked like I felt—rusty with a cracked windshield. I questioned if I could conduct a good interview, being fired had undermined my confidence in many ways.

I drove a few miles to the industrial area outside Fredericksburg, where the new building for the Thurman

---

3   Carolyn Custis James, *The Gospel of Ruth* (Grand Rapids: Zondervan, 2008), 97.

Brisben Center stood. Lemon cleaner scented the tidy hall-way, and hand-painted wall murals brightened the entry by the receptionist's desk, which had a monitor for security cameras. Was it scary to stay here?

I introduced myself to the receptionist, who called Bunny on the intercom. In a few moments, Bunny arrived to escort me upstairs to her office. Bunny offered me a chair and then sat behind her desk to explain how the facility operated.

The center, Bunny explained, had eighty beds. Individual stays capped at ninety days. The shelter also provided counseling, helped with job searches, and offered money-management courses, GED classes, and substance-abuse support programs.

"More and more folks are coming here due to the failing economy," Bunny said. "Many have lost jobs. Some paid their rent but the landlord didn't make the mortgage pay-ments. A few critically ill people have tried to get in, but we can't take people if they can't walk and bathe themselves."

I imagined being sick with no one to care for me and no place to go.

A center employee named Carolyn entered Bunny's office. "There's a new guy downstairs. He has two teardrop tattoos under his eye. He said one is for his father, who died in 2007, and the other is for his sister, who died of a brain tumor. Are we going to let him stay?"

Bunny paused, but then said, "Let him stay."

After Carolyn left, Bunny explained, "We've got to be careful that no symbols of gang-related violence come in. Prison inmates often tattoo teardrops to signify gang deaths."

Bunny's job of determining need wasn't easy.

"Some people come to the shelter due to unfortunate circumstances. They can't get out of the downward cycle without assistance. But there aren't many places they can go for help."

Gratitude arose in me for how supportive all my friends and family had been.

Bunny added that the program was not a free ride. "Everyone who stays here has to get a job and save money. They need to comply with any medications they're on and obey curfew."

"How do you protect people here?" I asked.

"I screen potential clients with telephone interviews and confer with police," Bunny said. "We deny housing to anyone with outstanding warrants or a history of sexual misconduct or violence. I also administer Breathalyzer tests."

"The program certainly seems thorough," I said. "How do you determine need?"

Bunny nodded. "That's not always easy. One time a seventy-eight-year-old woman told us she had $250,000 in the bank but didn't want to spend the money on food or shelter."

Bunny added, "Another time, a man came into town to collect the inheritance from his grandfather's estate. He wanted to know if he could spend a few nights at the shelter. I told him, 'We are not a free hotel.'"

I smiled.

Carolyn returned and took me to meet a few clients. "I found a few who are willing to interview with you," she said.

As we entered the cafeteria, I saw a woman and two men sitting at one of the tables. Shaking their hands, I introduced myself and sat with them.

"I really appreciate you being willing to talk with me. I got fired two months ago. Now I'm trying to figure out what to do with my life."

They sat politely and waited to hear more.

"You see, I have this dream of writing a book to encourage other people going through a hard time. I was hoping you might be able to help."

One of the men introduced himself as Bernard. In his late twenties, he looked strong and wiry. He had dark skin, a mustache and goatee, and a diamond stud in his left ear. "I just got here this morning. Ain't got nowhere else to go except the street."

Bernard said he had a job until his only sibling died. "When I was still trying to cope with that, my dad passed. When my mom died a little later, I went into a deep depression." Bernard's pain and confusion showed in his eyes. "If it wasn't for this place, I'd have to sleep on the street tonight." He covered his face with his hands.

The young woman introduced herself as Alli. This pretty girl's light brown hair was rubber-banded in a ponytail and her stomach was as round as a pumpkin. "I got hooked on drugs and that led to me losing custody of my kids. I bounced from job to job." Sadness crossed her face. "I met a guy, and he seemed nice but then things got abusive. I ended up on a friend's couch, three months pregnant. We couldn't afford to pay the bills. When my friend got foreclosed on, I came here."

Kevin, stocky with broad shoulders, was the second man. His brown face featured two dimples and an electric smile. At thirty-three years old, he'd been in the shelter for three weeks. "My marriage went rocky, and my wife set me up for psychiatric treatment. Things fell apart. I lived with my mom and her boyfriend for a while, but then they asked me to leave. I decided to stay here at the shelter till I can get back on my feet."

"I hated the thought of living in a homeless shelter," Alli said. "I figured it was going to be horrible. But everybody here cares. I've gotten more help in the last two weeks from total strangers than I've ever gotten from anybody else."

Bernard leaned forward. "This morning, when my friend called the shelter, I actually cried. I thought, *I'm too good for this place*. But I know God led me here for a reason. I've just got to open my eyes to see it."

Alli smiled at me. "He sure wasn't like that earlier today when he first arrived."

Bernard shrugged. "God's gonna tell me my purpose when he's good and ready. In the meantime, I'm not so bad off. At least nobody here makes me feel like a zero."

My heart was about to burst. These three strangers, who had every reason in the world to despair, drew strength and encouragement from each other. There was no hint of condemnation, only compassion.

"What advice would you have for someone who's going into that panic stage?" I asked.

"It helps to have a strategy," Kevin said. "I tell myself *when* I get back on my feet—not *if*. Before a door closes, I always have a Plan B."

"Sometimes you need a Plan C," Bernard said. "I chose the fast way to success, and that was my downfall."

I didn't pry into details; he was trying to find his way.

"I used to think I was invincible," Alli said. "Like nothing bad could happen to me. I burned a lot of bridges and blew off my family and friends over stupid stuff. I would tell people to not take for granted what they have."

"The devil's on your heels twenty-four-seven," Bernard said. "You've got to find a way to break bad habits."

"I had some close calls on the street," Alli said. "You can get into some bad situations. It's hard not to just give up and fall back on old patterns."

Bernard squared his shoulders and sat up straighter. "Sometimes you have to block out certain realities in order to do what you need to do. I have a son, but I can't take care of him if I'm a mess."

Kevin's jaw clenched. "I come from a middle-class family, but I don't want to go running to my mom or grandma, begging for a pillow or a buck. This place has the resources to help me be independent."

"I have an aunt who's a reverend," Bernard said. "She helped me out some, but she was always asking me, 'What are you going to do when I'm gone?' I figured it was time I got out on my own."

Despite deep pain and brokenness, these people held fierce desires for independence and restoration.

"Ninety-nine percent of the problems in my life are the result of my own bad choices," Alli said.

Bernard looked toward her with kindness. "No matter what path you end up on, God says, 'Don't forgot about me. I want to help bring you back.'" He looked at me. "I figure the Lord sends trials and tribulations to open our eyes and realize he's not done with us yet."

Across the room, a young Hispanic mother juggled a toddler in a stroller and spoke Spanish to a restless three-year-old while she made calls on the pay phone. She gave the older child what looked like a red ball. The youngster threw it across the room. When it landed at my feet, I realized it was a shiny apple with one bite taken out of it.

That brought to mind the Bible passage about the first temptation in the garden of Eden. Today, we still willfully taste experiences that later make us flee in shame.

When Bernard picked up the fruit, Alli stared at it and said, "We've got to appreciate the little things in life because that's all we have."

Bernard's face looked sad as he threw away the apple.

I wondered how long it had been since Alli had seen her children. Mine were away at college and I missed them too.

"Miss Tracy," Kevin said, "I hope there's a section in that book of yours for *appreciation*. I greatly appreciate having a safe place here. With a clean bed and hot meals."

His insight reminded me of many blessings for which to be grateful.

"Thank you for helping me," I said, standing. "You've given me some great ideas. I wish you all the best."

Kevin stood to shake my hand. The others did likewise.

"Good bye and good luck," Alli said.

Walking to the parking lot, I reflected on what Kevin, Bernard, and Alli had taught me anew. They demonstrated that even in desperate circumstances, we all still have God and each other. With hope and a helping hand, we can pick ourselves up and move forward.

When I reached my husband's truck, I noticed the car parked beside me held an assortment of toys, clothes, shoes, and papers. That vehicle, which probably belonged to one of Bunny's clients, most likely held all of someone's worldly possessions.

Humbled, I realized my situation was good indeed, even if I didn't have a job yet. I wouldn't take my furniture for granted, nor would I be embarrassed any more by the old rusty truck.

As I started the ignition, I thought of Luke 12:22–24: "Do not worry about your life, what you will eat; or about your body, what you will wear. Life is more than food, and the body is more than clothes. Consider the ravens: They do not sow or reap, they have no storeroom or barn; yet God feeds them. And how much more valuable you are than birds."

Just as God protected those in the shelter, he also cared for me. I did not need to worry. He would provide.

On the way home, I splurged at Dairy Queen's drive-through window to buy an ice cream cone. The $2.17 investment returned crunchy chocolate topping covering smooth vanilla cream. I savored my treat, acknowledging how blessed I was. I had a husband who loved me, a nice home, and reliable transportation. I had hope.

God gave abundantly, and he could restore any loss if I would only seek him.

Alli, Kevin, and Bernard had affirmed that a way forward was possible, no matter how far one fell. Like the sturdy building protecting them from the street, God shelters us during loss and hardship.

Lord, I prayed as I resumed the drive home, *for your name's sake, strengthen the hearts of those in the center. And help me commit to showing others the love of Christ.*

STUDY SCRIPTURE

For the eyes of the Lord range throughout the earth to strengthen those whose hearts are fully committed to him. (2 Chronicles 16:9)

STUDY QUESTIONS

1. Discuss a time in which you hit rock bottom. How did being around other people help you recover?

2. List four blessings that God has provided for you.

3. Discuss the difficulties you face. Ask others for strategies that they have found effective in overcoming. A pastor or librarian also may be able to refer you to resources that could be helpful.

4. Has someone ever called you by the wrong name? How did that make you feel? What do you suppose is God's reaction to his name being used in profane expressions?

CHAPTER SIX

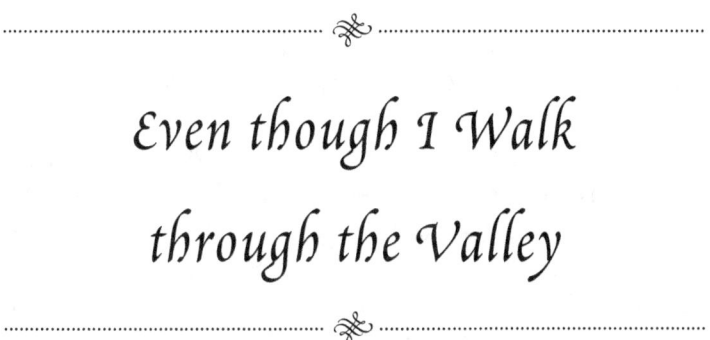

Even though I Walk through the Valley

Showing God my devotion seemed simple when activities included attending church on Sundays, tithing, and participating in small-group Bible studies. Trusting him with my unemployment required more faith, particularly when Lundy told me that the hospital had closed the job I was interested in due to funding concerns.

Equally difficult was obeying three summers ago, when God told me to go on a medical mission trip to Mongolia. Like joblessness, wilderness camping outside a remote village wasn't my idea of fun, particularly when the site was 6,400 miles away in a country where I didn't know the language or a single soul.

So I balked. "God, you know I will be faithful to any work you have *here* for me."

He said, "Go."

"Why me?" I whined. "Isn't there someone else who can do this?"

I continued to argue with him, even during the team meeting finalizing preparations at a local church. In the middle of one of my silent complaints, Jennifer, one of my teammates-to-be, leaned toward me and whispered, "Tracy, when I was praying for you just now, I got a picture of a donkey in my mind. Does that mean anything to you?"

I disliked the notion that God saw me as a stubborn mule. No longer could I let my fears be an excuse for disobedience.

Ken, Jennifer, Jenny, Emily and I navigated three flights during thirty-three hours to see the image of Genghis Khan wave from banners decorating the airport of Ulaanbaatar, capital of Mongolia. Tom, the American missionary who had requested help, picked us up. He had served in the military and still wore his salt-and-pepper hair cut short.

We rested at an apartment loaned to missionaries, then met our Mongolian counterparts at their church to coordinate details for the children's summer camp, health clinics, and English classes we planned to offer. Mostly the five of us just smiled and nodded, because we couldn't understand anyone other than Tom.

The next morning, with a total of four hours of sleep during the last two days, we tossed luggage into vans and drove north six hours through rocky terrain sparsely tufted with clumps of dry grass.

A herd of seventy-five unattended camels broke the monotony as they stared at us curiously from the side of the road, chewing their cud.

At one point, we passed an overturned car, with debris scattered all around it. I suggested we check to see if anyone needed help, but the missionary said we couldn't stop.

As he drove on, the awareness of our vulnerability and isolation heightened. We had only a satellite phone for emergencies.

After bumping over clay and rock roads until our brains rattled in our heads, we arrived at the river campsite outside Eruu, City of Blessing. Shamanism dominated the region.

Our Mongolian partners had arrived earlier and set up camp. Four tents—two for men and two for women—flanked the *ger*, which was a large, portable Mongolian home. The round structure accommodated up to thirty people and served as our classroom. Nearby was the village's rustic hospital, powered by one dangling strand of electric wire and intermittent bulbs. The only latrine facilities consisted of two wooden outhouses with ten-inch oval holes in the floor. The toilet paper arrangement was strictly bring-your-own.

Mountain ranges miles away encircled us. The open plain had dry brown vegetation sprinkled with green blades for the sixty-day summer. An aromatic ground cover crackled under our feet as we walked.

During this season, the sun rose around seven. Temperatures reached ninety degrees as early as eight, with no relief from the heat until after nine p.m., when the sun set.

Wooden stockades protected the village of three thousand people from marauding animals. At night, domestic animals remained inside the fences. During the day, we heard sheep, pigs, goats, horses, and cattle meandering toward the river below the bluff where our tents were. Sunlight burned brightly over the steppe, and the only trees reposed a quarter mile away at the fork of the fast-flowing stream.

As dusk approached, Chimgay (all Mongolian names are spelled phonetically here for convenience) built a fire and set over it the huge black kettle that would be our only pot for cooking. She was my age, and her father lived in the village. Chimgay owned a restaurant in Ulaanbaatar, and at the camp she organized and cooked meals for at least twenty-one people three times a day, with no refrigeration available.

Her willowy figure moved like clockwork around the kitchen tent, her silken black hair, threaded with silver, tied back loosely in a ponytail. Her culinary skills turned bits of meat, carrots, cabbage, and noodles into delicacies that attracted many guests—some welcome, some not.

A few members of the latter category crept into the campground our first night. I awakened from a fitful sleep about eleven. Shadowy figures moved around the kitchen tent, and I heard strange snuffles that told me animals were after the food. If the animals ate our supplies, we wouldn't have anything to eat. However, we had been warned that rabies was a problem.

I hated to wake anyone, but didn't want to go into the unknown alone. I woke Jennifer, who slept to my right. "Something is in the kitchen eating the food," I whispered.

Her sleepy eyes opened wide. "What are we going to do?"

"C'mon." We left our bedding area and got a couple of sticks from the firewood pile. I hit the kitchen tent's outer flap with my large branch; Jennifer whacked the canvas with another one. We heard animals rush out the other side.

Pointing our flashlights inside, we looked around. When we were sure the place had been vacated, we entered and picked up the scraps that had been left by the canine scavengers. We covered the refuse so that no more problems would occur that night.

We turned off our flashlights and let the stars illuminate our way as we wearily trudged back to our tent, where Gwen, a nurse from another church, Jenny, and her teenage daughter, Emily, slept peacefully. Moving like gymnasts, Jennifer and I stepped over the occupied sleeping bags and wriggled into our spots.

As I lay awake, I prayed, *Thank you, God, for getting us here safely and for protecting us.*

The smell of burning wood awoke me the next morning. Chimgay had risen before dawn and started a fire to warm milk tea, which was the Mongolian national beverage. Someone from the village rode a bicycle to our kitchen tent each morning with a metal container of fresh milk.

Chimgay's resilience astonished me. She never complained; she never even appeared tired.

"Did you see where animals got into the food last night?" I asked as I approached.

Her brow furrowed. She pointed to the fire and pantomimed putting food into her mouth. Obviously she had no idea what I'd said.

Conversation was going to be a challenge. The Mongolian language evolved from a hybrid of Russian and Chinese, which had few sounds or letters similar to English. The only person fluent in both languages was Tom.

After breakfast, our team assembled for the morning devotion. Tom led in Mongolian, then translated in English. Quoting from Isaiah 40:6–8, he said, "All men are like grass, and all their glory is like the flowers of the field. Surely the people are grass. The grass withers and the flowers fall, but the words of the Lord stand forever."

Our group discussed the frailty of our bodies but the eternity of our spirits. We talked about what in our lives would have lasting value. Tom juggled translating as the conversation flowed.

Following breakfast, many children arrived from the village. Curious, they wanted to see what we were doing. We led them in games and invited them to watch skits. Tom translated the Bible stories I acted out. The children laughed and clustered closer to hear more.

Around lunch, the children went away so we could eat privately. We didn't have enough resources to feed them all.

Some of the children went to play by the river. We thought nothing of it until a panicked girl ran back up the hill.

The Shadow of Death

The girl rushed up the slope, yelling to the Mongolian women on our team. We Americans couldn't make out anything being said, but we knew there was trouble.

Chimgay gestured wildly toward the river, and another woman stumbled down the bluff toward where the children clustered on the edge of the water, watching deep whorls spin in the furious current. The Mongolian women shouted for help. A frantic search began along the shore, accompanied by frenzied yells.

From body language, I understood that a child had gotten caught in the stream and gone under. The other kids couldn't find her. No one knew if the girl remained trapped below the surface or had washed downstream.

More people arrived to help, and search parties raced down the river's bank. For more than forty-five minutes, everyone worked feverishly to find the girl. Villagers came as the news spread.

Our missionary group stood along the high edge of the stream and prayed. I knew that God was going to do a miracle. Why else would he have orchestrated our medical team's arrival for that very day?

An old pickup careened toward the river, leaving a trail of dust in its wake. Men in uniform jumped out. The crowd looked to one older man. This leader asked something, and the others shook their heads. The man sent a diver into the blue hole. The swimmer dove down and resurfaced several times. Finally he came up holding a girl's limp body.

The doctor and nurse from our team rushed over to the inert shape on shore. I couldn't watch. I closed my eyes and redoubled my prayers. *Oh, Lord, have mercy!*

When next I looked, men carrying a stretcher toiled up the hill. On it was a body shrouded with a white sheet.

God, why did you bring us here only to see death? I cried out in my heart.

That second night in our camp was somber. No one spoke, but sniffles could be heard throughout the area.

Sobbing discreetly in a private corner, I opened misty eyes to see an older woman from the village watching me. Earlier in the day she had brought fresh yogurt and tart berries as gifts for the doctor for helping a family member. The woman looked at me oddly, as though she were trying to figure out why an American stranger cried over a Mongolian child.

Because Chimgay had gone to comfort the family of the dead girl, and the other Mongolian women on our team were distraught, I finished dinner. Open-fire cooking wasn't in my repertoire, but if someone didn't step up, the team would go hungry.

No one seemed to have any appetite, except one heavyset Mongolian teammate who had recently converted to Christianity. He struggled to recognize that the purpose of the trip was to serve rather than be waited on. This man sat on a stool like it was a throne and stared at me while I worked. He gestured displeasure that the dumplings weren't being made right. Was he really that shallow?

Spoonfuls of sticky dough boiled in the cauldron. The puffy mounds made me think of the girl's white-draped body. I recalled a sentence I'd read in a book about a Nazi concentration camp when author Elie Wiesel had also questioned God about injustice and the loss of an innocent life. Wiesel had written that the stew tasted like dead bodies to him on the night that guards hanged a young boy.[4]

Despite my silent disappointment with God, I comforted the nurse, Gwen, as she relived each moment of trying to save the girl. "Never in all the years I've taught CPR have I had to try to save a life," she said. "The doctor told me to go ahead because I knew more about how to do it than he did."

She hugged her knees and shivered. "I thought we had a chance to save her because the water had been freezing cold. I put my lips onto hers and breathed. I got my hopes up when I saw her slender chest rise slightly, but then everything gushed out from her stomach. I can't get that taste out of my mouth." Gwen sobbed.

"You did everything you could," I said, scooting over to her and wrapping my arms around her. I held her for a long time.

The rest of the night, I argued with God. *Why didn't you do a miracle?*

But he chose silence.

Morning dawned with anxiety. Would the villagers hold us responsible? Were we in danger?

The team gathered in a circle for devotions. Tom led us in prayer, then asked if anyone wanted to say something. The group shifted uncomfortably and remained quiet.

"How are we supposed to show these people God's love when the second day we're here, someone dies and we couldn't save them?" I asked.

No one met my eyes or spoke. In a full-fledged crisis of faith, I doubted God's goodness.

Finally, one of the young Mongolian men, Ganbuyer, spoke. His face showed deep peace and confidence. "In devotions yesterday, we read about people being like grass. Our time in this world is short. How will we spend the

---

4   Elie Wiesel, *Night* (New York: Bantam Books, 1982), 60, http://www.msgr.ca/msgr-8/LENT_holocaust_e.htm. Last accessed 25 June 2010.

life we have remaining to ensure that the word and glory of the Lord go forth?" Tom translated each word with precision and compassion.

Ganbuyer's rock-solid faith secured me and his gentle demeanor reassured me. I had traveled halfway around the world to learn that God was with us, even in death. All of us would die. Our time on earth was limited, and we seldom had warning that the end was near. What we chose to do with the now was critical.

Our team prepared as best we could for however the day might unfold. We sang a praise song that Tom had translated and taught to the Mongolians. The lyrics said to honor God when the sun is shining as well as when there is pain.

The day proceeded peacefully. Children arrived at nine for games and Bible stories. Some parents accompanied them, but there were no recriminations about the drowning. The adults just wanted to be reassured that their children were safe and that someone was watching them.

At lunch, we had two new guests. One was a malnourished boy of thirteen who looked like he was six years old. Our doctor had seen the boy at the clinic and recognized classic signs of famine. The boy's pinched-thin face had a triangular shape, and his wrist bones fit inside the circle formed by my index finger and thumb.

With downcast eyes, the boy perched by the kitchen tent. Ganbuyer piled food on a plate and passed it to the boy. We all crowded shoulder-to-shoulder at the folding table, seated on small plastic stools. An unfolded black plastic garbage bag mounted on two poles and attached to Tom's minivan served as a sunshield.

The second guest was a battle-scarred male dog with rottweiler bloodlines. Matted fur covered the animal's gaunt frame. Half his nose and the right side of his upper lip were missing, presumably from a fight. Despite the dog's damaged appearance, he commanded respect. Other dogs stayed far away as long as this one presided over the camp. Chimgay rewarded his vigilance with leftovers. The partnership satisfied all, except the pack that had to scrounge for food elsewhere.

The scarred dog adopted and protected us. He even let us pet him, although those first attempts were done gingerly. We named him Scruffy.

By the third evening, I thought things had settled. I was wrong.

Emily, a cute teenager with braces, freckles, and long brunette hair, came back from the outhouse and said, "A puppy is trapped in the hole under the toilet floor. I heard it whimpering and I saw it below the floorboards. It's only a few weeks old."

Tom conferred with our Mongolian teammates. They shook their heads and cautioned against taking action. Apparently, the Mongolians put unwanted animals in the large trash container or underground toilet holes to die from starvation or dehydration. That was their method of population control. While cruel according to American standards, for the Mongolians, the decision was necessary. Food to fill human bellies would be scarce during the long and brutal winter. No sense prolonging a life that wouldn't be useful. Accepting that cultural practice was bitter.

Throughout the rest of the third day and into the fourth, none of us wanted to go to the outhouse. But necessity forced the issue because no other private area existed. Each trip to the outhouse sickened me. The thought of that puppy trapped in a muck of feces and urine was unbearable.

By the fourth evening, the cries of the trapped puppy had grown weaker, yet each time it heard footsteps, it whined hopefully for help. I broke down and sobbed loudly the whole way back to the tent. Tsatsa and her fiancé, Ulaanaa, looked at me with concern.

Collapsing on my sleeping bag, I asked God why he'd brought me to this place in which I was useless. Physically, I was exhausted. Mentally, I was broken and completely vulnerable. I fell asleep smelling the Mongolian "incense" of dried livestock dung, which they burned to keep mosquitoes at bay. The wall of smoke did nothing to dispel the sting of my despair.

In the morning, Scruffy snored beside our tent. He was louder than the men. Walking past the dog, I noticed something black and white snuggled near him. The ball of fluff was the puppy from the outhouse!

During breakfast, Tsatsa and Ulaanaa greeted me with beaming smiles. I found out that they had gone back to the outhouse late at night. Ulaanaa had rigged a noose of rope and lifted the puppy five or six feet through the narrow hole in the floor. Then they washed the puppy in the river.

Their act of kindness symbolized to me what God has done for us. Although we were covered in filth, his love rescues and washes us clean. An incredible joy rose in me.

The puppy bounced over our feet under the breakfast table, looking up expectantly for a treat. She appeared no worse for her ordeal. I marveled at her resilience and will to live.

Camp routine continued. We had devotions and worked with the children. Frisbees, boomerangs, kites, and soccer balls littered the campground.

In the afternoon, some of the team went to help an elderly lady weed her garden. I accompanied Chimgay to pay respects to the parents whose daughter had drowned.

Back at camp, heat beat us down. A few Mongolian women decided to wash clothes in the river. The cool water looked inviting—even though we knew of its treachery. Hovering close to shore, we rubbed our clothes with a plain bar of soap and rinsed in the stream.

That simple, time-honored task shared with women filled me with fellowship and contentment. I was thousands of miles from home, but I wasn't alone. God was everywhere. He loved his people and tended them. He watched over all of us with a shepherd's eye. Not even physical death separated our spirit from him.

Nearby, a Mongolian woman dipped her long, black mane of hair in the stream to wash. Across from her, two horses stood knee deep. The bay rested its head on the back of the dappled gray and dozed. The gray didn't seem to mind. I could lean on God's shoulder and gather strength too.

Back at the campsite, I copied the Mongolian women and put the clothes to dry on herb groundcover. A pleasing, spicy scent arose.

Ken practiced English with some young adults in the *ger*. "I'm fine. Thank you for asking. How are you?"

I crawled into the tent to rest during the blistering hot afternoon. Even though the inside felt like a sauna, at least there was some respite from the sun's merciless rays.

With evening came relief from the heat, but a new threat presented. Across the horizon, a massive storm was building. Lightning crashed across the sky, and the wind raced toward us. We had nowhere to go. Tom had taken the van that morning to visit another team working farther north. We hoped the storm would skirt us. It didn't.

Hitting like a sledge hammer, torrential rain blew into us. Our tent strained on its tethers. Five of us grabbed support poles, praying that our combined weight would anchor the canvas. Emily looked terrified.

"Lord," I prayed loudly, "we trust you. We know that whatever happens, we can count on you. You are the master of the universe. We ask you to protect us."

Emily looked calmer, but the storm was far from done. One of the men yelled for us to go into the *ger*. That was the only structure in our camp with no metal. We scurried inside the portable structure, where the Mongolian women cowered. The men secured the generator and other loose items, then joined us.

I felt total calm and peace. I don't know why. Maybe so much had happened that I was numb. Maybe I had finally crossed over to a place of complete trust in God, even if that might mean the end.

I remembered watching a woman fly a kite earlier that afternoon. As the kite soared high on the stiff breeze, God had said to my spirit, "I make some people like kites. They only fly in the strongest of winds." I wanted to be one of those people he released to rise above difficult circumstances.

The storm's fury finally passed. We wearily returned to our soggy tents and worked together to re-stake the poles.

In my quiet prayer time, God told me, "Daughter, I am teaching you endurance." He seemed to think I could make it; I had doubts.

Simple routines emerged over the next few days. We went through daily rituals, drank milk tea, and ate noodles for almost every meal.

During one devotional time, Tom said, "Yesterday's faith is not adequate for today. We need to look to God for the grace to continue working."

Exhaustion took a toll, and each activity became rote. Classes for the children. Afternoon rest. Help cook supper and clean. I had barely enough strength to do the next task.

The rescued puppy chased a soccer ball, rolled by the malnourished boy, who helped where he could. He shooed away curious cattle wandering around while Scruffy snoozed in the shade of a tent. We were a band of misfits, yet the blend was harmonious.

Ulaanaa played his guitar and started throat singing, an ancient Mongolian art that originated with shepherds far from family. To entertain themselves, the solitary guardians developed a type of music performed using only vibrations of the vocal chords. No words or lip motions were made. Each unique sound represented something. One chord would be the river; another, the sky. Ulaanaa trilled a song that Genghis Khan's soldiers might have heard.

In a modern context, Gwen showed some women how to knit. Colorful skeins of yarn wrapped around their arms as they practiced.

I rounded up Magda, the teenage Mongolian boy on our ministry team who was the son of the overweight man.

We walked a mile to a house in the village to draw fresh well water. After Magda and I filled the heavy metal canister, we struggled to carry the load back to camp. He and I each held one side.

Two small children, perhaps six years old, noticed our plight. With no prompting, they skipped over to us and got on either side. Their small hands grasped our free ones. Then the children stepped and leaned outward. In doing so, they shared and lightened the burden. I'll never forgot that lovely gift. The children saw a need, even in strangers, and willingly helped.

As our trip neared the end, I grew concerned about the malnourished boy, Scruffy, and the puppy. The boy's lethargy had disappeared; Scruffy's coat was sleek and full; the puppy's life had been saved. But who would feed them when we were gone?

I found the missionary director for a private conference. "Tom, how can I help support that boy?"

"I can't think of a way to do anything."

"What do you mean? Can't we set up a fund at the hospital where someone sees that he gets food?"

"Corruption is rampant here," Tom said. "There's no way to ensure the money won't be redirected. I'll do what I can for him every time we come back."

I couldn't evacuate the dogs, either. Even if I could afford the international air-freight charge, rabies quarantine required months of seclusion before placement.

Stewing over these limitations, I noticed a pack of dogs growling and snarling on the edge of the village. A pack of males pursued one female in heat. Had we saved the puppy only for a worse fate?

Railing at God in my heart, I demanded to know why he had asked us to come here. Was it right for him to let someone feel warmth, a sense of belonging, and a full belly for a short while—only to be abandoned?

Feeling guilty, all I could do was count down the days before my return to "civilization." We had two days left, but my precious supply of toilet wipes numbered only three sheets. I missed fast food and indoor plumbing.

Across the field, a young, bony woman herded sheep as she wearily carried a three-year-old child. Thinking the mother and toddler were probably thirsty, I took a cup of water to them. Getting closer, I saw the child had green nasal discharge—sure sign of an infection. The little one's cheeks flushed with fever. All of our medicine had been used. My frustration mounted.

But the mother's gratitude for one cup of water humbled me.

God spoke quietly in that encounter. He answered the nagging question I had barraged him about for days about helping a short time, only to leave everyone when I returned to the United States. "Daughter," he said to me, "it is better for these precious ones to know at least some of my love and joy than to pass this earthly life with neither."

I was astounded. The God of the universe heard my challenge and countered with a message of love. He didn't berate me or hit me with a thunderbolt for questioning his plan. Firmly and gently, he called me to show goodness to others, even if for a brief period. Compassion revealed the glory of God, and no kindness was ever wasted.

My vanity had expected miracles on the scale of life resurrected, epic battles won, or astounding healings. Prior to this moment, I had been blind to one of the most amazing feats of all: ordinary humans setting aside selfish agendas to show God's goodness in the midst of a regular day.

Later, in the privacy of our tent, Emily shared her last piece of chocolate candy with me. On my pillow rested a crayon picture of a purple horse with an orange mane given in farewell by one of the Mongolian children.

These simple, but profound, treasures reminded me of God's provision. He could make a few fish and a loaf of bread feed thousands. I should not worry about a job; he would ensure my care.

STUDY SCRIPTURE

Again Jesus said, "...do you truly love me?"
"Yes, Lord, you know that I love you."
Jesus said, "Take care of my sheep." (John 21:16)

STUDY QUESTIONS

1. Describe a situation in which you were supposed to serve others but you didn't want to. What resulted from your obedience—or your failure to cooperate with God's leading?

2. Discuss a time when someone modeled unconditional love to you.

3. Examine why "shepherds" must have a love relationship with God before they can effectively care for the flock.

4. Do any shadows of guilt or shame hang over you? If so, how can you be freed from them?

CHAPTER SEVEN

I Will Fear No Evil for You Are with Me

When I got home from Mongolia, I put that pony picture on my fridge. For years it has reminded me of God's principle of kindness. Now, even with a job loss, God was keeping the icebox full.

As I opened the refrigerator to grab a snack, the phone rang.

"Hi," my friend Mary said. "How would you like to go with me to a meditation center for yoga on Saturday?"

I knew nothing about yoga. But I did know that Mary followed Buddhist beliefs. Although I loved my friend, I needed to qualify my requirements for the outing. "Mary," I said, "you know I can't be chanting BuddhaBuddhaBuddha."

Mary giggled. I breathed a sigh of relief that she wasn't offended.

We had the type of friendship where we could be candid with each other. Throughout the years, she and I had shared several adventures. Mary was a lot of fun.

One time, she took me sailing on her small boat in Colonial Beach. We ate peanut-butter sandwiches and practiced turnabouts along the shore. Stiff winds made the waves choppy. Pretty soon, I turned green and recycled my sandwich overboard. Mary never once complained that I'd ruined her sailing day.

She'd also served as the wedding coordinator when Dan and I married. Even though the Christian ceremony was held in a church, she never intimated any discomfort. She honored my values and stood beside me as a friend; I wanted to do the same for her.

However, I didn't want to find myself in a position that compromised my beliefs. So I called my pastor to run the yoga idea by him.

"I'd advise against going," Pastor Dale said. "You could be opening yourself up to bad influences. When we pray, we speak to someone. In Psalm 19, the Bible says, 'May the words of my mouth and the meditation of my heart be pleasing in your sight, O Lord, my Rock and my Redeemer.'"

I saw his point but still wondered.

Dale ended our conversation with "Pray about it. Then you'll know what to do."

Even after prayer, the direction remained opaque. I knew Mary would understand if I didn't go. But curiosity kept nagging. I didn't want to stay huddled in some cozy Christian circle, to the exclusion of investigating how others experienced faith. In the final analysis, I believed God loved me enough to protect me and allow me the intellectual freedom to explore. So I went.

My sense of security slipped as I drove farther into the wilderness past Bowling Green. Mary and I chatted during the drive. I told her about some of my concerns, and she listened patiently.

She told me about the class she was teaching on women's issues. "I have four brave men attending it too."

"That's great. I wish I could attend a class to learn about guys. Maybe I could improve communication with my sons."

"This week, we discussed a case of sexual harassment involving multiple charges against a male administrator at our school," Mary said.

I admired the risk she took to allow a public discussion about a sensitive topic, encouraging her students to tackle tough issues.

After several turns on country roads, Mary and I approached the entrance of the meditation center. A rustic three-story hotel stood in front of a concrete building. Despite my bravado, when I walked into the shabby conference room, I feared I'd crossed the boundary of good sense.

Five-foot-wide pictures of white-turbaned Indian men with dark mustaches and goatees stared at me. A low ceiling closed me in, and the musty room smelled like unwashed clothes. The few windows offered little light. What had I been thinking when I told Mary I'd go to a meditation center in the boondocks?

Mary greeted and hugged a woman named Donna, who had invited her to the center. They worked together as teachers. Mary introduced me to Donna. Mary and I took off our shoes and tiptoed to the far end of the room, where an instructor lectured. The large man had an athletic build like a football player. He addressed a group of twenty-five students visiting from Donna's yoga classes. The young people listened quietly.

I tried to keep an open mind. I wanted to learn about how the brain works in relaxation techniques, but without subjecting myself to religious rituals opposed to mine. I hoped that would be possible here.

"Habits become our mental program until we override them," the instructor said. "We can't stop negative information from arriving into our minds, but we can adjust how we respond. When we think, speak, and act differently, we have the potential to remap the whole human being. By using self-talk we can reprogram the mind and literally create new neural paths."

Donna appeared in the doorway and announced that lunch was ready. We all put on our shoes, left the building, and followed the sidewalk, littered with pine needles, toward a cafeteria. Students lined up along folding tables to fill soft tacos with bean spread.

A skeletal-thin lady with sunken cheeks ladled soup into bowls. When I reached the desserts, my mouth watered at the sight of cherry cobbler. Not seeing any pieces that were already on paper plates, I served myself from the metal pan. Skeleton lady glared at me.

"Sorry," I said.

The grim woman moved from her post by the soup to guard the cobbler, indicating her disapproval of my initiative.

Mary and I found a table in the corner. "My burrito is cold," she said. "Do you see a microwave?"

"Why don't you ask that guy pouring the carrot juice?" I suggested. The tall, thin man looked like a hippie with his long, gray ponytail wrapped over his shoulder.

Mary declined to ask. She ate the cold food, mumbling under her breath. I was glad I'd eaten a large breakfast.

The young adults didn't seem to mind the chilled vegetarian fare. Black beans disappeared at the same rate as green alfalfa sprouts. Students talked in muted tones.

After lunch, we returned to the front of the conference building, where a guide waited to take us to an indoor labyrinth for a meditation exercise.

We walked to a round structure about thirty-five feet in diameter. Thirty people crowded inside and sat on folding chairs around the circumference. Above chest-high plywood walls, wooden spokes supported a high ceiling that had one window in the center of the roof. The place resembled a Mongolian *ger*.

On the floor, a painted tarp had circular designs like a race track with eight lanes. However, the lines curved mid-section and turned ninety degrees into random directions. In the middle, a dove held a branch with green, heart-shaped leaves. A shiny yellow background highlighted the bird. The outer edges of the mat had colorful symbols representing many faiths: the Christian cross, the Jewish star, the Native American medicine wheel, the Muslim star and crescent, and the Chinese yin and yang.

Our middle-aged guide, Julia, wore an olive green blouse and dark brown corduroy slacks. She spoke softly, with a South African accent. "A labyrinth is one winding path, with no dead ends and no tricks. Unlike a maze, a labyrinth is not about finding a way out. A labyrinth leads us inevitably to the center. Along the way, we learn to release and be fully present."

I relaxed with her soothing tone and clear explanation.

She said that labyrinths became popular in medieval times when Christian believers wanted to make a pilgrimage to the Holy Land, but they couldn't because of dangerous conditions between Europe and the Middle East. "Some people created designs on the floors of cathedrals to symbolize this religious journey instead."

My spiritual quest in visiting a yoga center seemed similar. I hungered to know God more.

"This exercise is a pilgrimage to the heart of self through a higher power. Let go of linear thinking. Allow the deeper part of you to work through things."

Julia explained three phases in the labyrinth exercise. First, participants would release distractions to be fully present in the moment as we began the path toward the center, where the dove was. Once in the center, we would receive insights. Finally, we would walk out with a new awareness of self and others.

Julia gave an example of a transaction: entering the path with anger issues, standing at the center to receive grace and blessings, and returning with new ideas for conflict resolution.

Her gentle voice was repeatedly obscured by the sound of guns firing at a military installation in the distance. I thought about the irony of a meditation center proximal to a firing range.

This dichotomy of peace and war resembled the thoughts often competing in my mind. Although I wanted to be in harmony with ideals of generosity and kindness, these often clashed with my selfish desires.

Julia urged us to move in silence and take turns along the lanes. "Proceed at an easy pace. There's no hurry, and no right or wrong way to do this."

Groups of three started at the entry and walked the lanes. The room was quiet, except for a gentle instrumental background. Over the music a soft voice chanted, "Walk with me. Be my guide through the darkness into the light."

When it was my turn, I looked at the floor so my feet wouldn't step into someone else's path. With only six inches width per lane, the fit was tight.

I prayed as I walked. *Okay, God. I'm here seeking you. Please show me what I can learn today.*

I didn't hear any bells or whistles. No "oms" or "ums." I followed the lane, gaining confidence as I figured out the pattern. Then, without warning, the path hooked. Frustrated, I felt off balance. A spark of fear crept in, even though I was only walking on a painted mat.

This meditation exercise was a metaphor for life. Just when I thought I was going in the right direction, the road suddenly changed. Having been fired, I found myself somewhere new and had to trust God to show me where to go next.

I doggedly pursued one twist and turn after another. I became dizzy and tired. *God, I want to be close to you.*

Twice I sidestepped a spider crawling along the floor. Despite the small space and constant movement, each person in the room purposefully dodged the defenseless little creature. Crushing it would have violated the reverence of the moment.

I felt just as vulnerable and insignificant as that eight-legged arachnid. Would I ever get to the center?

In the midst of my doubt God said to me, *You are the center of my heart.*

Although I was far from where the dove rested, I received a huge insight. God was with me on the journey . . . because he loved me. My exact location was less significant than the fact that I sought him.

For the next few laps, I savored the feeling of being precious to him.

Once in the center, I examined the dove. I felt that anything after the love message would be anticlimactic, but I was wrong. God had more to say. As I scooted to free up space for four others in the center, God said, *There's room in my heart for more. I want you to tell them!*

Tears welled in my eyes at this unexpected development. I felt full and complete.

Journeying back to the start, I wondered how to share this incredible love with those around me.

Then I saw a curious thing. Somehow, the determined spider had not only made it to the center, but it had spun a strand from the ceiling. It dangled right over the dove, as though the spider wanted a front-row seat to watch the pilgrims.

A couple of girls shrank back from the spider. A young man wearing a day-old beard calmly walked up to it and swept the strand up high. He safely transported the spider on its bungee cord to an outer area with no traffic.

As the young man resumed his walk, a cute girl in a short, plaid skirt rewarded his heroics by bumping him and smiling.

After all the participants had finished, Julia said, "Walking together created a sense of community, even though we went in separate directions."

She was right. That exercise illustrated that although we each walked our own individual path, we gained by sharing the journey.

Energized by the interfaith exercise, I was ready for the next one.

My glow of anticipation didn't last long. As soon as we got back into the dingy room, Donna asked if anyone minded having his or her picture taken. I raised my hand.

"I'll just crop her out," the photographer said, taking a picture fully toward me.

Why wasn't my request for privacy respected? I turned backward on my mat so that my feet faced the opposite way of everyone else as we started warm-up exercises.

"Hey," Mary whispered. "You're going against the current. You're interrupting the flow."

I wanted to be a good guest. However, the photographer was lighting up the room like the Fourth of July with all the flashes. My nonconformist self dominated. "I'll turn around after she stops taking pictures," I said loudly.

"The peace and tranquility inside us," Donna said, "is louder than all other sounds."

I wanted that to be true for me. But then a man's voice boomed from the far end of the room, "We have to overcome the mind's chatter. That's how one man had more than seven hundred incarnations in one life."

Good grief. That's crazy.

The man's imperious discussion of incarnations creeped me out. One of the Indian men in the giant poster smirked at me. The photographer continued to prowl up and down the rows of students.

Donna's sing-song voice called, "Feel the energy flowing through us. Relax your mind in the stillness. Place your hands and feet on the floor and surrender to the pose."

Again, the man's voice interrupted. "The intellect wrecks your spirit. The third eye is in the middle of your forehead."

What kind of gibberish was he dishing out?

I gave up doing any stretches. Any notion of feeling safe evaporated.

Donna instructed us to get into a position called "Happy Baby." Mary lay on her back, her legs extended to the ceiling, with her toes pointed toward her head. She seemed to be having difficulty, so Donna walked toward her and whispered into her ear.

"Oh, you mean play with my toes," Mary crowed as she tickled her feet with her fingers.

I laughed out loud. The sight of a grown woman playing with her feet in a position I could never have achieved, even with aspirin, was hilarious.

The loud man left the room. The place became so quiet I could hear the ticking of the wall clock.

The instructor concluded with a prayer pose. I was glad to leave. Outside the building, I noticed the same loud man talking to a young woman who listened intently. I wondered how the information about incarnations would affect her.

Following the students to the parking lot, I thought about how young adults must sift through many ideas to determine their own religious beliefs. Mary asked what I thought of the experience.

"Did you hear what the guy said about incarnations?" I asked.

"No," Mary said, "I heard the commotion but not exactly what was said."

"How can somebody have seven hundred incarnations?"

Mary launched into a coherent differentiation between our faiths. "Christianity and Buddhism are mutually exclusive. One believes in heaven; the other in reincarnation. In Buddhism, you'd better get life right the first time, or you could come back as an inchworm."

I stifled a laugh, wondering if she were serious. "I don't understand why people would follow Buddha as a god."

"Buddha was a guide, not a god," Mary said. "And Buddhism is a philosophy—not a religion."

I wondered how she could follow a belief system that called for perfection, with no guarantee of achieving such a goal. I had made many mistakes in my life. My only hope of attaining some heavenly afterlife was to rely on the mercy of a loving God. I couldn't stand the thought of multiple reruns to get things right. I certainly didn't have any interest in being an inchworm.

I wanted to know I was going somewhere special, and when I arrived, someone would greet me with loving arms. I didn't want the end of my physical life to be a cosmic jeopardy game in which I drew a short lot for reappearance as a slug or gazelle.

Mary couldn't answer all my questions. She too was a sojourner seeking truth.

"Mary," I said, "when you coordinated my wedding, I never thought about how awkward a Christian setting might be for you."

She shrugged. "I figured I'd be all right. After all, what were they going to do? Cut me in pieces and sacrifice me?"

Although Mary meant to be funny, her comment reminded me of what had happened that morning when I'd visited my old church for a yard sale. I hadn't been back since my divorce years ago, because the memories there were too painful. But they were raising money for Christian missions in Haiti, and I wanted to do my part.

My anxiety diminished when I received a warm welcome from George and Joan, who had remained steadfast friends despite the rupture of my first marriage. Their unconditional acceptance restored me.

However, not all church-goers modeled George and Joan's tenderness. Across the gym, an elderly lady called to me from her Christmas-ornament table. "Hey, Tracy."

Flattered to be remembered, I walked over, anticipating another nice reunion.

"Where do you go to church now?" she asked without a smile.

I had barely responded to that question before she launched another grenade. "Do you ever get to see your boys?"

Mission control: we have a hit. This lady had no idea how the breakdown in communication with my sons had devastated me following the divorce.

She stared at my left hand, where I wore Dan's wedding band. "Did you marry again?" Contempt dripped from her thin lips.

I knew I'd failed miserably in my first marriage. But God had given me a second chance. This woman's heart had no room for forgiveness. Her bitter example contrasted greatly with the gentleness my friends had shown me.

Which type of Christ's church did I represent? Did I model Christ's true love to others by being inclusive and welcoming, like George and Joan? Or did I push people away, judging their circumstances and choices without fully understanding their situations?

If my Buddhist friend Mary had suffered from "antagonistic Christianity," I could understand how the idea of becoming an inchworm would seem preferable.

God's personal assurance during the meditation exercise confirmed that I was at the center of his heart. Despite all that he knew about my shortcomings—those I'd already committed as well as the ones yet to occur—he desired me. He hadn't abandoned me.

And he had specifically told me to let others know that he had room for them too. I mentally committed myself to doing that, one footstep at a time.

I looked at Mary and smiled; her friendship was true. We would continue to walk together and engage in respectful conversations for growth.

"If you really keep the royal law found in Scripture, 'Love your neighbor as yourself,' you are doing right" (James 2:8).

STUDY SCRIPTURE

Whether you turn to the right or to the left,
your ears will hear a voice behind you, saying,
"This is the way; walk in it." (Isaiah 30:21)

STUDY QUESTIONS

1. What key facts differentiate Christianity from all other religions?

2. Write about a time when you faced a fork in the road. Describe how the choices took you onto new paths of discovery—either positive or negative.

3. Describe a time when God clearly spoke to you about what direction he wanted you to take. How did you respond?

4. Imagine having to walk down a dark alley alone at midnight. How does your outlook change if you know a 240-pound NFL middle linebacker walks with you?

CHAPTER EIGHT

Your Rod and Your

Staff Comfort Me

L oving our neighbors seems easy, at least when the other people look attractive and act nicely. But what do we do with marked differences, particularly unpleasant ones?

From November 2007 to December 2008, I taught GED classes to young men in a remote maximum-security facility. Locked away in that job, I learned how faith overcame fear.

I went to the bedroom closet and retrieved my prayer journals that covered the time I worked in jail. Maybe reviewing those lessons would help me find more strength to sustain in this period of uncertainty after getting fired.

Teaching high-school inmates was another unexpected jaunt on my faith walk. I prayed God would provide opportunities for glory and prestige. He did open doors. But not the ones I expected.

With the perspective of time, I saw that God's answers to my prayer directed me to service instead of self-gratification.

As I settled back in my favorite chair to read my journals, I recalled what my life was like back in the fall of 2007. My divorce had been final for a year, but my sons still felt torn between loyalties and kept their distance from me. I had been out of work since July after completing two semesters coordinating student activities at the local university. Overconfident, I believed another job would come easily. Three months of fruitless searching indicated otherwise.

October 27, 2007

I asked the Lord tonight how I can get my heart to thaw. I don't trust anyone.

Moments after that prayer, I read this in the Bible: "I will give them an undivided heart and put a new spirit in them: I will remove from them their heart of stone and give them a heart of flesh" (Ezekiel 11:19–20).

Coincidence? I don't think so.

November 7, 2007

Had the interview for the GED job at the correctional facility today. Concertina wire lined the top of the twenty-foot-high chain-link fence. Inside, the facility was bright and clean, but the small space was suffocating. Not sure how well I'd do there if I got the job.

I feel a weird sense of time warp, as though I'm waiting for something. But I don't know what.

November 9, 2007

Having another confidence crisis today! Wish I wasn't afraid of failing. Why can't I just laugh and be jovial and breeze through everything confidently? Instead my eyes are red from crying. Lonely, I worry about money and never finding my purpose in life. The truth is, I feel incapable of accomplishing anything important.

November 10, 2007

Another day of solitude. No family to welcome home and no job to visit with co-workers.

Felt led to read Matthew 25:34–40: "I was thirsty and you gave me something to drink; I was a stranger and you invited me in. . . . I was sick and you looked after me; I was in prison and you came to visit me. The king will reply: 'I tell you the truth, whatever you do for one of the least of these brothers of mine, you did for me.'"

God seemed to use this passage to indicate he desired my service at the prison.

November 15, 2007

"Hold what is within your hand and do not doubt or look beyond." Twice last night I awoke with this comment on my mind. Both times it felt like a strong command from God, telling me to take the prison job and not hesitate anymore.

Dear God, if the job is offered to me, I'll take it. But you know that I won't be sad if no one calls about it either.

November 29, 2007

Finished my third day at the correctional high school. Alternated between crying in fear and laughing out loud.

Dread descends upon me each morning as I enter the compound and hear the double metal doors slam behind me.

The students and I are locked in a room to which I do not have a key. Guards patrol the hallway and scan classrooms through glass windows lined with wire. I wear a radio on my belt so I can call for help should assistance be needed.

Other staff warned me to be aware of "stinging," which was when a resident exposed himself. That was a creepy aspect I'd never considered as a job risk.

A guard also cautioned me that a female instructor at another facility had recently been gang raped. Could that happen to me? I can only fully rely upon God.

This place is full of dichotomies. For example, two students acted like they were going to get in a fist fight, then one quipped, "Guess we need to call Dr. Phil in on this." They laughed at each other, then walked down the hall.

In the middle of a discussion on the merits of a diploma versus a GED, the students performed an impromptu rap song. One line went something like "...went to ask the lama." Genius that I am, I said, "Oh, do you mean the Dalai Lama?" They laughed heartily, then explained that *lama* was slang for a gun.

God's promise to be my rod takes on new meaning in this setting. Rods were clubs that shepherds used in biblical times to keep predators away from sheep.[5] Without God's rod of protection, I am defenseless against young men who are larger and stronger than I am.

I also depend on kind coworkers who inspire me as they patiently teach me about this strange culture. Despite our bleak surroundings, the employees here have welcomed me and seem to care. Like embodiments of God's wooden staff to lead sheep, my coworkers are guiding me.

December 10, 2007
I heard the F word more times this morning than in all the rest of my life. No one directed the cuss word at me; that's just how the students converse.

One student asked me, "Do you know who you're in here with? There's a reason we're locked up." He was trying to intimidate me, but God held me in his palm.

"I realize that," I answered. "But there's no guarantee of safety outside that fence, either."

5   David H. Roper, "Through the Valley," *The Power of His Presence: A Year of Devotions from the Writings of Ray Stedman*, compiled by Mark Mitchell. http://www.RayStedman.org. Last accessed 25 June 2010.

Another student asked, "Do you know you're in here with males in their prime who are going to look you up and down since they don't get to see other women?"

"Yes, I do," I said. "But that happens on the outside of this facility too. My hope is that at some point you will see me as a person. I want to learn about you, and maybe there'll be a thing or two I can teach you that will help you."

The sincerity and lack of fear in my voice seemed to satisfy them because they didn't barrage me with any more questions.

At home, I got a phone call from a guy named Dan. My neighbor Donna, playing Cupid, gave him my number. She and Dan were close friends, and she thought that he and I would get along well.

December 12, 2007

Today I accompanied staff members beyond the school into a pod, the inmates' housing area. Here during the day, guards monitor prisoners in an enclosed recreation room containing only a television, tables, and chairs. Nearby, tiny cells cordoned off with metal bars hold beds where the inmates sleep at night.

During a counseling session in the pod while I observed staff talk with one inmate, an alarm sounded. Guards had found another prisoner in his room, lying in a pool of blood. The young man had stabbed himself with a fork. The thought of such desperation saddened me.

After work that night, I watched my younger son wrestle on his high school team. The announcer introduced him as a senior, then gave the names of his parents—but my name wasn't one of them. *Had my son's dad already remarried?*

The principal, for whom I had worked five years, looked at me apologetically from across the gym. Somehow, I found the composure to wink at him to show that everything was okay. Everything *wasn't* all right. But at least I managed to internalize the blow without breaking down in public.

This deep hurt reminded me of what a long-term staffer told me earlier in the day: several of our inmates were sexually abused as youngsters—some as young as eight years old. The parents of one of our inmates gave their son to homosexual prostitution in exchange for drugs. Pain at being estranged from my younger son paled in comparison to what those men have endured.

I've resolved to convert my yearning for my sons into a deep compassion for other young men. Parenting doesn't have to be limited to biological offspring.

December 15, 2007

After the end of my first marriage, God called me to an intimate time with him for restoration and rebuilding. For three years during separation and legal proceedings, I've battled loneliness and the desire to find companionship and affirmation in another man's arms. But God encouraged me to find solace in his embrace instead, and not to short-circuit the process of deep self-examination.

I do not want to stay single forever. As wounds from my first marriage healed, I began asking God to send me another partner.

When I felt certain that God wanted me to serve at this prison, I prayed, "God, I'll do this for you, but could you please send someone to help so I don't have to go through it alone?"

I don't know if there's a connection here, but I had my first date with Dan today. Could his frank blue eyes and balding head be the answer to my prayer?

Our initial encounter was straightforward. We met at a restaurant for lunch, then went shopping—jeans for Dan and classroom posters for me. In that brief time together, he showed constancy and compassion. Perhaps this relationship will eventually be able to restore my ability to trust.

December 16, 2007

"Go, stand in the temple courts and tell the people the full message of this new life" (Acts 5:20). This passage references an angel releasing Jesus' apostles from jail, where they'd been imprisoned by jealous religious leaders. I too have been freed from a prison of bitterness over broken relationships. The story of how God's love saved me needs to be told to others bound in pain.

December 18, 2007
Previewed the *Scrooge* movie for school tomorrow. Marley's ghost said, "This chain I wear is one I forged link by link." I hope I can help these young men see how past choices may be binding them and how they can change this pattern. I also wonder if I can alter my behavior to become healthier—spiritually and emotionally.

December 23, 2007
My workday began with the art teacher blowing soap bubbles as students entered the school building from the pods. Another teacher moon-walked down the corridor. Their joy flashed brilliantly across the bleak backdrop of the off-white block walls.

We staff members tried to offset the grief many of our students feel about spending a Christmas in prison, far away from loved ones.

January 1, 2008
"The Lord will surely comfort Zion and will look with compassion on all her ruins; he will make her deserts like Eden, her wastelands like the garden of the Lord. Joy and gladness will be found in her, thanksgiving and the sound of singing" (Isaiah 51:3).

After years of turmoil, I feel peace in my heart. God is healing the deep brokenness of loss and helping me discover who I am. Not only can I work in a prison, but I also can touch lives there with gentleness and kindness.

January 2, 2008
The head of school security is a man in his sixties whom everyone calls Daddy Fi. He's always dressed immaculately in a suit and tie. Though wiry, he carries a lot of weight

around the prison. He led a prominent gang in his youth. He uses that inside knowledge to mentor young men who seek to define themselves the way he did years ago. Now a strong Christian, he has a reputation for fairness.

Daddy Fi told me today that a beloved nurse was murdered at another clinic by an inmate whom she called *son*. "You absolutely cannot trust the prisoners," he said. "Believe the best, but don't *ever* let your guard down."

It seems that every time I start to feel secure, something erodes that notion. I find it exhausting to always be alert for danger, trusting God for protection is the only way I can carry on.

January 4, 2008
I still wonder sometimes if where I am is real. It feels strange to say good-bye to the old me and embrace the ever-emerging new one. God as my shepherd has led me with his staff to a flock I never imagined.

Each day at the prison, I've learned that fear bows in the face of candid confrontation. I choose not to be afraid, and my students sense that. They seldom test me now and show more respect for the information I teach.

Many of the students have had little formal education. Most started living on the streets by sixth grade. Their pride is fierce.

I plan lessons to meet their hunger for knowledge in a way that balances with their limited reading skills. Today we evaluated calories on a fast-food menu, combining math and nutrition. Yesterday, we raced matchbox cars to demonstrate Newton's laws of motion. I work against the inertia of their past to show them that they can succeed.

I address each student by the title "Mr." with his last name to show respect. I want to build their identities as educated men.

They honor my firmness. Progress is being made. And yet, some of the male staff have doubts. One told me I was too soft to last at the prison.

I confessed to Daddy Fi, who has become a trusted advisor, that I might not measure up to the task.

"How you gonna be weak when the Spirit of God Almighty is in you?" he asked me, looking into my eyes. "People thought Jesus was weak when he didn't save himself from torture, mockery, and death. But that despair was a gift—not impotence."

Daddy Fi's counsel greatly impacted me. With God as my advocate, how can I fail? The Lord of the universe provides a hedge of protection around me. I have no need to fear.

March 23, 2008

Lord Jesus, you are master of death and life. You have given me breath and resurrected hope and dreams. Help me have strength to continue following you and watching your miracles and triumphs, even in the darkest moments. Please help me, in humble word and deed, testify to your truth, constancy, and love. Amen.

March 27, 2008

I feel inadequate. Today at school, I told one of my students, Mr. R, that he was being a turd. I was fed up with his rudeness and refusal to work. He ignored me.

I also told Mr. M that he wasn't dumb and that wasting his mind was pitiful. He kept distracting others and did everything possible to disrupt instruction. The saddest part is that he is probably one of the brightest students I've had in all my years of teaching.

Mr. M and Mr. R teamed up to drive me crazy by commenting with sexual innuendos. To drown out their remarks, I read poetry loudly.

Mr. M perked up for a minute and said, "Poetry always makes me feel better."

"Oh," I shot back, "do you want me to quit so you can stay depressed?"

A glimmer of a smile touched his lips.

Later, Mr. R said he'd just had his fourth birthday in jail. Mr. M told me his "shorty," or girlfriend, had written to say she was pregnant with another man's baby.

I realized then that their acting out reflected deep pain that they didn't know how else to release.

March 28, 2008
First block today was science, and we're studying the rock cycle. So I brought in three types of mud I'd bagged from the woods, and real seashells, so the students could make fossils. They kept saying they were playing in sh**. I dryly retorted it was my present to them.

They sat like angels during the video about rock formation. Afterward, one student pronounced, "Yo, it'll take three weeks to count to one million—and that's how many years that dude is saying it takes to make a rock."

I smiled; learning was happening.

In the second block, Mr. O planted lima beans in plastic cups filled with soil. I connected this gardening experiment with the novel *Seedfolks*, which tells how a community garden transformed an inner-city ghetto.[6] I marveled at the tenderness with which Mr. O tucked white beans into the black soil.

March 29, 2008
I attended a women's forum today with my long-time friend and teaching mentor, Susie. I told her that God was using the jail job to hammer me into steel.

She agreed and added, "He's training you to fight with character and integrity from a deep inner core."

Susie's comment solidified that the prison job was shaping me in positive ways.

April 1, 2008
April Fool's jokes abounded. After lunch Daddy Fi told the principal that all the teachers had the flu, so he

---

6   Paul Fleischman, *Seedfolks* (New York, NY: HarperTrophy, 1997).

cancelled classes over the intercom. All of us staff members giggled when we heard the announcement, but we still dutifully stood by our classroom doors ready for the afternoon session.

April 2, 2008

For the anatomy unit, I set a plastic skeleton in a classroom chair and propped a sign in his hand, saying, "Welcome to class."

When Mr. P came in, he sat next to the skeleton. "Hey," he said, grinning at me, "this is how long your class lasts." Looking at the skeleton, he added, "I feel your pain, dog."

April 3, 2008

On my way to work, I asked God to show me if there was any part of myself that I withheld from him. He answered in my heart, *Give me your ambitions.*

Wow! That convicted. I've never thought of myself as prideful, but that was part of my resistance to the job at the prison—not enough prestige. Yuck. I hate it when God shows me my shortcomings.

In the middle of the afternoon class, a guard unlocked the door and took Mr. S for transport. S had been planting lima beans, and his eyes filled with fear. He had no idea where he was going—or for how long.

He left behind a notebook wrapped in newspaper. I wondered why.

The assistant principal later told me S had been removed for protective custody. He'd been targeted by a gang within the pod where he slept. I figured that notebook must have been his protection against a "shank," a makeshift knife.

April 4, 2008

Mr. G ripped his GED practice essay into shreds. He said the topics were stupid. I challenged him to write a satire to mock the assignment. I told him a proud mind could disagree, but only a brilliant mind could persuade the other side to see a new perspective. He considered that for a moment and his anger subsided, but he never did get on task.

Got a new student today; he said his religion is vampirism. A staff member later explained that the young man uses that line to act crazy and keep bigger inmates away from him.

Mr. L crushed the live asparagus fern on my desk and asked, "Why is this rough?" He seemed oblivious to how his heavy touch destroyed the plant.

Mr. H threw a banana up and down in the air at least fifty times, saying each time in a high-pitched falsetto, "I'm doing my class work."

Neither of these students got on track today. They left the classroom discussing wet dreams.

Lord, how can I keep trying to reach them? Sometimes, the situation seems hopeless.

April 13, 2008

In my quiet prayer time today, I heard this from God: *"Tracy, pray over those young men as though they were your sons. They shall be redeemed. Go forth in boldness and push back the darkness. I will equip and heal. I will save."*

This insight came as I prepared a lesson connecting the tattoos branded on Jews during the Holocaust to gang insignia the prisoners give each other in the pods. They use "needles" out of staples and ink from printer cartridges stolen from the supply closet.

I want to help these young men find identities beyond the gang labels others have bestowed upon them. In class we watched a scene from the end of the movie *Schindler's List* in which Schindler cried because he realized that selling his watch could have purchased and saved many more Jewish lives from Nazi brutality.

"I know about power over life and death," Mr. G said. "I had a bead on this dude standing in the doorway of his house, but I didn't shoot because a woman stood right behind him holding a baby. I didn't want to take a chance on hitting them."

I could only imagine the moral complexities Mr. G already had faced at his young age, and I was glad that this class reminded him of his ability to choose compassion instead of violence.

April 15, 2008

Mr. Y was back in class today after thirty days in "lock," which is solitary confinement. He sang an obscene rap.

"Please don't," I said gently but firmly. He stopped.

He stared at my chest for a long time. "Are those crosses on your blouse?"

I looked down. "Yes, I guess they are," I said, seeing the *t* threads in a new light. God shielded me as surely as though I wore armor.

Mr. Y started a grammar practice test. Soon, I noticed him looking at his palm. Blood oozed out. He must have stabbed the pencil tip into his skin.

When he got up to show me his wound, I noticed his shirt was dirty, with food on it, and the collar was uneven. He held out his hand toward me like a child. "That hurts like a bit**," he said, towering over me.

I had an urge to fix his collar, wash the sleepy crust from his eyes, and tell him everything was going to be okay. But any physical touch upon these isolated, lonely young men was ill advised as it was subject to misinterpretation by them as romantic interest. I looked at him with compassion and radioed Daddy Fi to take him to the clinic.

Evening fell as I read these old journals. How God had blessed me! He had used joblessness then to break my pride so that I would be willing to take a job of service. In that new position, he secured me in a place full of danger and entrusted me with opportunities to minister to young men battling for hope.

God had also given me a second chance for a marriage based on faith. Dan epitomizes a steady love that cares for me in the best and worst of times. His unconditional love is much like my heavenly Father's.

God is trustworthy. He will never abandon or forsake me—even if I do let my own sense of self-importance get out of control.

God used my prison experience to emphasize the value of humility. The satisfaction I felt in service there rivaled any fleeting accomplishment that could be applauded by men.

Glamorous titles dimmed next to the glory of God's call to serve others. "I have set the Lord always before me. Because he is at my right hand, I will not be shaken" (Psalm 16:8).

My current situation included joblessness again, and maybe more lessons about pride, but that didn't imprison me from discovering aspects of growth that God wanted to reveal. Just as he had kept me safe in a volatile work setting, he would help me navigate finding my next purpose and place to serve.

STUDY SCRIPTURE

As a prisoner for the Lord, then, I urge you to live a life worthy of the calling you have received. Be completely humble and gentle; be patient, bearing with one another in love. Make every effort to keep the unity of the Spirit through the bond of peace. (Ephesians 4:1–3)

STUDY QUESTIONS

1. Describe a time when you were blinded by the lime-light of a particular job and missed out on a more fulfilling ministry.

2. Think about any selfish ambitions you may have. How could "jailing" those desires resemble being "a pris-oner for the Lord"?

3. What Scripture has someone quoted to you that sus-tained you through trials?

4. In an agrarian society, a shepherd uses a stout wooden rod and staff to protect his flock. What tools are available to you today to keep others safe from rejection and discouragement?

CHAPTER NINE

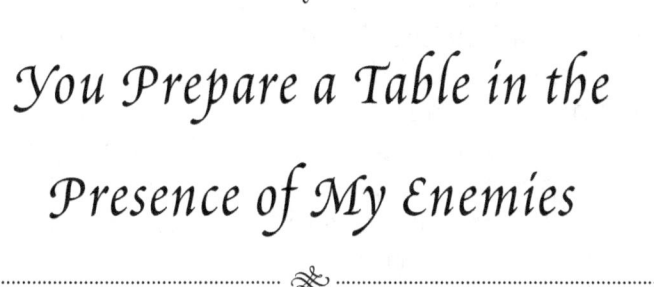

You Prepare a Table in the

Presence of My Enemies

Every November, the Marines celebrate their founding
with a birthday ball. Attending the event was part of
Dan's job, and would have been part of mine—had
I not been fired. We wondered whether or not I should
accompany him this year since the supportive-wife role
potentially conflicted with my persona non grata status as
a terminated employee.

My husband told me I didn't need to go; he feared I'd
be miserable. I understood his motivation and appreciated
his kindness. However, part of me wanted to wear the sexy
black dress I'd already bought for the event and prome-
nade on my husband's arm.

I decided to go and make the best of it.

A week before the formal, Dan came home from work and said, "I had a private talk today with one of the upper-level managers who sat in on your termination hearing. He intimated that your firing was a gut-punch by the human resources director to get back at me."

In spite of Dan's deadpan delivery, his shocking pronouncement at least explained my unexpected exit from the editing job. It would seem that the dismissal revolved around events other than my efforts to learn and contribute. The insight should have offered solace, but the stark unfairness just made me mad all over again.

Then Dan added, "You'll never guess who's assigned to sit at the same table with us at the ball."

"Who?" I anticipated friends from other sections or maybe my mentor, Jared, and his wife.

"Matt and his girlfriend."

That couple would be fun to visit with. "Who else?" I asked, knowing the tables usually sat several people.

"The director of human resources and his wife."

No way was I ever going near that creep again! John had used his position, and my vulnerability, to betray my request for help as a new employee within the organization. I couldn't believe that he'd manipulated my dismissal to injure Dan. Could someone really be that petty? I couldn't understand anyone with an attitude that callous.

How could I be expected to break bread with the instigator of my firing?

"What do you want to do?" Dan asked.

Swallowing my irritation, I wondered if this might be a God-given opportunity to demonstrate growth and grace.

I had been studying that adversity revealed the heavenly royalty in us. "We must leave the prison behind to enter the palace. People of royalty focus on who they are called to be. They have forgiven those who have hurt them. . . . They don't live in the bondage of prison but in the wholeness of the palace."[7] This quote by Kris Vallotton and Bill

_____
7   Kris Vallotton and Bill Johnson, *The Supernatural Ways of Royalty* (Shippensburg, PA: Destiny Image Publishers, Inc., 2006), 49.

Johnson in *The Supernatural Ways of Royalty* challenged me to think about blessings instead of losses.

After all, I was a daughter of the Most High King, who had showered me with mercy and forgiveness. He expected me to extend what I'd received to others. I wasn't sure I could do that with the people who had fired me. But I knew that's what my Lord desired.

It's easy to be regal when everything is coming up roses. The real test is what we do when the thorns prick us. Did I have enough of God's love in me to behave like a mature child of the King in the presence of my enemies?

I wanted to tell Dan that I was so imbued with God's love that I could handle that seating assignment with grace and dignity. But I kept visualizing being seated next to a coiled cobra and having to smile and make small talk so my husband wouldn't be mortified.

After several moments of reflection, I said, "I can't sit there and pretend that everything's okay. I can be polite. But I won't be fake."

Dan respected my feelings and I had confidence that he would find a solution to whether or not I should go. I left the final choice with Dan.

All weekend I wondered what he would decide, but I didn't badger him. On Monday morning, he e-mailed me from work, saying that our seating arrangements had changed. We'd been moved to another table.

Though I wanted to believe I could have handled such a tense situation gracefully, I was relieved that I was not going to be tested after all.

Reading the Bible later that day, I found comfort in God's Word.

Because of his great love for us, God, who is rich in mercy, made us alive with Christ even when we were dead in transgressions—it is by grace you have been saved. And God raised us up with Christ and seated us with him in the heavenly realms . . . that in the coming ages he might show the incomparable riches of his grace, expressed in his kindness to us in Christ Jesus. (Ephesians 2:4–7)

The next night, I hooked Dan's bowtie around the white, starched collar of his shirt. His blue eyes met mine in the mirror. We smiled. Whatever happened didn't matter because we had each other.

I shimmied into the evening gown and did a twirl or two to watch the satin fabric swirl. Dangly rhinestone earrings sparkled against my neck. My sandals matched the black beading on the dress straps. I felt beautiful and joyous. Whatever was ahead, I could handle it.

Dan put on the tux jacket, and we drove to the club for the ceremony.

As soon as I entered the ballroom, I saw Karen, my former supervisor. The three of us were the only ones who'd arrived so far.

Great, I thought, *now I have to face her too.*

I had not been able to forgive her for knowing about the termination and not having the decency to talk with me about it. Her betrayal hurt more than John's.

Dan excused himself to find a restroom; great timing on his part.

Okay, God, you've got me here. Now what?

Karen stood in the corner with her back to me, fiddling with a camera. I felt sure she'd noticed my arrival. Was she avoiding me? Should I go talk to her? If I did, could my tone be kind and respectful?

Taking a deep breath, I walked over to her and said, "Hi, Karen, how are you?"

She pivoted on her heels. Her face contorted with a mixture of emotions I couldn't read. After a fleeting moment, she resumed a passive expression and said, "Fine, thank you." Then she strode away.

I wasn't prepared for that reaction. I had hoped we might be able to talk and find closure to the firing episode. Apparently, her feelings were even stronger than mine.

I found that odd, since I was the one who'd been fired. Perhaps my comments at the termination hearing had resulted in supervisors reevaluating their expectations of new employees. At the hearing I had said that the absence of standard operating procedures, clear deadlines, and style manuals negatively impacted new editors' abilities to meet expectations.

Other guests came in. I lingered in a corner, waiting for Dan. When he returned from the bathroom, I told him what had happened with Karen. A minute later, she walked up to us. "Would you like a photo together?"

"Sure," we both said simultaneously. I knew our picture would never appear in any company publication, but I appreciated her gesture.

My first test passed, Dan and I entered the dining hall. Chandeliers beamed upon linen-covered tables with centerpieces of fresh flowers. Women in elaborate dresses clustered around one another like colorful bouquets. Marines wore their dress blues, the handsome uniforms fitting like gloves. Scarlet stripes, signifying the shed blood of brethren, ran down the outer seams of navy-blue trousers. Black tunics showcased rows of service medals. Every object symbolized something, including one table with upside-down dishes, to show respect for fallen comrades.

The honor guard entered, with minutely measured march steps, in time to the drum cadence. A trumpet sounded the call to attention as a huge birthday cake on a trolley arrived, escorted by white-gloved Marines. One Marine used his sword to cut the cake. The oldest Marine present took a piece of the birthday cake first, then gave the next slice to the youngest Marine. This exchange represented passing the legacy of honor from one generation to the next.

We watched a video message from the commandant. The film began with a scene of a drill instructor yelling to new recruits, "Get off my bus!"

I had felt that way when told I was being fired.

The script showed other vignettes. "Motivation is like a cup of coffee," said one Marine in the video. "It lasts about one hour. But inspiration lasts a lifetime."

I wanted to do what was right, but often lacked the initiative or follow-through to sustain my good intentions.

A man in the film said he was related to a young Marine who had died protecting an entry gate from an enemy-driven truck laden with explosives. "Every moment of his life led up to those six seconds in Ramadi."

In my "six seconds" of proving my true character, would I demonstrate courage? What would I be willing to sacrifice when everything was on the line?

If my Christian walk weakens or fails, I could destroy others' belief that rescue and redemption are possible. Conversely, when I confidently conduct myself as a royal descendant of the King, I model strength and hope for those who might otherwise falter under life's burdens.

"What will you do to carry out that legacy of valor?" the general challenged in his closing. "How will you honor these traditions as you go forward?"

There I sat in the presence of people who had recently fired me, analyzing my motives. Why had I come here? Was I driven by pride? Or was I just stupid? Mostly, I wanted to prove that I could take a hit and keep standing. I long to show everyone that instead of cowering in a corner, I was flourishing. My identity came from more than a job title or paycheck. My heavenly Father loved me and provided everything I needed.

When those managers banished me from the basement, they freed me to pursue new dreams. I should be grateful. My job loss didn't destroy me; instead, it strengthened my faith, because I saw God sustain me time and again. Just as God had protected me in Mongolia and at the prison, I could continue to count on him.

I had overcome. My "six seconds" of battle had resulted in metamorphosis, not catastrophe. Peace filled me like never before.

What can be done to someone who trusts in God and has learned to face fear head on? No bullets can penetrate that shield.

After finishing my dinner, I left to find the restroom. As I wound through the crowd, I passed the director of human resources. John smiled at me. From somewhere deep inside, a genuine smile rose to my lips. To my surprise, I felt absolutely no rancor toward him.

When bad things happened, I'd chosen to trust God. One job had ended; others would be available in the future. I was in a season of education, and part of the lesson was discovering my heritage as a favored child. That realization freed me from haunting self-doubts. I sailed through the ballroom, holding my head high.

Another quote from *The Supernatural Ways of Royalty* came to mind: "This is the true mentality of a prince and princess. They spend more time raising up people around them rather than worrying about their own significance. They already know who they are inside, which enables them to become selfless and give out more than they receive."[8]

When I got back to the table, Dan looked at me with love. The disc jockey played music for a slow dance. My husband held out his hand and led me to the dance floor. He took me in his arms, and we swayed back and forth. In his clear gaze, I saw acceptance of the total me—including my temper, pride, courage, and vulnerability.

The legacy I want to carry forth isn't military brilliance or physical feats; it's love. I want to share with others how much God values them. Horrible disappointments herald beginnings, not endings.

Dan leaned forward to brush his lips across mine. That felt so good we kissed again, right on that dance floor in

---

8   Vallotton and Johnson, 77.

front of all those people. Those tender smooches sealed a chapter and healed a heart.

A few days later, Dan and I attended a holiday performance by the community symphony orchestra. The auditorium was decorated with red poinsettias and evergreen wreaths.

I loved the way this annual event brought together people of many ages and backgrounds. On stage in the violin section, a college student with long blonde hair shared a music stand with a grandmotherly matron in a beaded jacket. In the audience, parents with rosy-cheeked children sat next to frail residents from a nursing home. We all joined together to celebrate the season.

Musicians entered the stage and began to tune their instruments.

"This is a very nice Christmas present," I said, snuggling next to my husband.

The house lights dimmed.

"I was afraid I was going to be fired today," Dan said.

Before I could respond, the conductor took the stage. Tubas, trumpets, and trombones gleamed in the spotlight. Vocalists sang in Latin as a church bell chimed in the background.

But I couldn't get Dan's brief comment out of my mind.

"God rest ye merry, gentlemen, let nothing you dismay. For Jesus Christ, our Savior, was born on Christmas day . . ."

As the choir sang that song, spotlights created a rainbow around the musicians, and a blue background with white snowflakes danced around the stage. The conductor's baton skipped merrily with the music, and his tuxedo tails swished back and forth, keeping time. I sensed Dan's body relax.

The high-pitched notes of a recorder reminded me of the sound made by a jewelry box my younger son had given me one Christmas. He'd saved coins to purchase the gift at a yard sale. This tender memory stroked my heart as softly as the notes from the piano.

Violins and oboes joined in. Then the piano played solo again, concluding with a touch as gentle as a mother's hand upon her newborn. Electric guitar strings wound up, bringing to mind sleds racing downhill with wind-blown riders squealing with glee.

The music stopped, and the spell-bound audience sat in silence for a moment, as if disappointed that the magical interlude had ended. Then applause exploded. House lights came up.

As we stood, I whispered, "How long have you been worried about being fired?"

"All day."

"What's going on?"

"You know that new product we've been working on day and night for the last few months? Well, we managed to get it finished on time. But we got complaints from the field that it's not right."

"Dan, I know you and your team. You would only turn out the finest work. Just because somebody doesn't understand how to use your product yet, that doesn't mean the quality of your work won't be vindicated in time."

"That doesn't mean I won't get fired. After all, look what they did to you." Apparently what happened to me had eroded his confidence in the fairness of the organization.

"Dan, there are worse things than being fired."

"Like what?"

"Like staying in a place that kills your passion. Where no matter how hard you work, you get kicked in the stomach every day."

His eyes met mine; he saw I wasn't afraid.

"We have stuff we can sell. We can get by if we need to." From my own trials, I knew God would take care of us.

So often we cling to the familiar, but in doing so, we often miss opportunities for growth. I wanted to reassure Dan that hope existed.

We left the auditorium and walked down the dimly lit street to where our cars were parked. Shadows obscured

Dan's face. He looked down at the sidewalk, his shoulders slumped.

On the drive home, I wondered what I could do to bolster his confidence. I recalled hearing a story about Admiral David Glasgow Farragut. In 1864, Farragut participated in a naval attack. The lead ship hit an underwater mine; the fleet floundered. In that moment of crisis, Farragut uttered a command to charge forward, navigating right over the treacherous waters. His ship and the rest of the fleet passed safely and forced the enemy's surrender.[9]

While Dan watched television, I went into the bedroom and dialed his office number, waiting for the voice mail to connect. Knowing he'd get my message first thing in the morning, I said, "Dan, I love you. So damn the torpedoes, full speed ahead!"

I hung up the phone and turned out the light, knowing he'd get my underlying message that I believed in him and to move forward without fear because God would deliver.

STUDY SCRIPTURE

But the angel said to them, "Do not be afraid. I bring you
good news of great joy that will be for all the people.
Today, in the town of David a Savior has been born to you;
he is Christ the Lord." (Luke 2:10–11)

---

9 Chester G. Hearn, *Admiral David Glasgow Farragut: The Civil War Years* (Annapolis, MD: Naval Institute Press, 1988), 263–265. http://www.history.navy.mil/trivia/trivia02.htm. Last accessed 25 June 2010.

STUDY QUESTIONS

1. How can knowing that Jesus is the Savior bring us comfort?

2. What is a holiday tradition that you cherish? Do your family celebrations include God?

3. Think about how instruments performing together comprise a symphony. Read 1 Corinthians 12:12–31. How does this passage relate to individual talents?

4. What new song is God inviting you to perform for him?

5. Banqueting with enemies implies that hands hold food, rather than weapons. In your most vulnerable times, what keeps you safe?

CHAPTER TEN

You Anoint My Head with Oil

I stared at the stack of Christmas presents on the counter in the living room, ready to be sent to relatives who lived out of state. Dan had given me a list of who was to get what. My job was to match names with gifts, wrap everything in cheery paper with ribbon and bows, package them in cardboard boxes, slap on mailing labels, and take everything to the post office. Should've been fun, right?

Smack in the middle of this task, our mortgage banker called. We'd applied for a refinance of our home loan at a lower interest rate so we could better pay the bills until I could find new employment.

"I'm sorry," she said, "but you need income to qualify for refinancing your home."

"I had income until recently," I explained, "and we will again soon." Our current mortgage was only a year old, and we had excellent credit. We'd even made extra principal payments when I had the editing job in the military basement facility.

"I'm sorry," the banker repeated. "But regulations are really strict now. Your area has taken a hit on appraisals too. Some properties are less than fifty percent of values two years ago."

In my mind, I complained about banks loaning at a premium and leaving clients holding the bag when the market dipped. But none of my mental arguments changed a thing.

I slammed down the phone and fumed as I resumed my task, not near as excited about wrapping and packaging gifts as I had been. As a matter of fact, I was so upset that I mixed up some of the presents. After most of the boxes were sealed, I realized that I'd put two of the gifts in the wrong boxes. I ripped off the tape, muttering like a crazy woman. The Grinch would have been proud.

I switched contents between the boxes and started to tape the first one shut again. The tape dispenser screeched and ran out. My eyes rolled heavenward. My attitude plunged.

I finally loaded the boxes in the car and drove to the post office, hoping that if I got out of the house for a while, things would get better.

After taking my place in line, I noticed a display of tape dispensers on the wall. I set my boxes on the counter and picked one up. As I returned to my place in line, a woman stepped right in front of me. The nerve!

In a huff, I retrieved the stack of boxes off the counter and promptly dropped two of them. The lady who'd butted into line looked at me, but made no offer to help, in spite of my obvious predicament.

With an audible sigh, I rescued the dropped boxes from the floor and maneuvered in front of the lady, without even mumbling, "Excuse me." Silently, I dared her to say anything. She didn't.

From behind me, I heard her cell phone ring. "Hi. How are you? . . . I see . . . I'll pray for you."

Figures. What a great Christian witness she was, cutting in line and not bothering to offer to help someone. Of course, I was oblivious to my own poor example.

When my turn came, the uniformed woman behind the desk asked how I wanted to send the packages. "Regular mail," I said.

"We don't have regular mail."

"What *do* you have?" I didn't bother to hide the edge in my voice.

"Express, priority, and parcel post."

Parcel post? What in the world was that?

Figuring that express and priority had to be more expensive, I said, "Parcel post, please."

"That will take three weeks for delivery."

I did a quick computation. No way would our packages arrive before Christmas. They might get there in time for New Year's Eve.

The line behind me grew longer. People moved restlessly.

"Anything over thirteen ounces automatically rolls up to priority," the clerk informed me.

I was certain all my boxes were over thirteen ounces. "Guess I'll take priority then." Anger rose within me. The postal service seemed to conspire to gouge people trying to send holiday cheer.

As the woman weighed each of my packages one at a time, I noticed she looked tired. Her neck flushed with stress as she moved the stack of boxes and took my payment.

Her mechanical voice repeated the same litany of delivery options to the woman behind me. I felt sorry for her. That job couldn't be easy.

With my errand accomplished, I moved on to the next item on my list. I drove to a discount store, where I planned to buy colorful wrapped candy to fill a glass vase for a holiday centerpiece. That sounded like something fun to relieve the stress of the morning.

On one of the store's shelves, I spied a package of red-and-white-striped soft peppermints. I squeezed the bag to see if the candy really was soft. *Not.* The round balls had atrophied into granite. Anyone who bit into those would end up with dentures. The expiration date was unreadable without my glasses.

The other merchandise looked junky, and I worried that any unnecessary expense would be too much. Disgusted, I left without buying anything.

The phone rang when I got home. I hoped the call would be a response to a teaching position I'd applied for.

"Hello."

To my delight, the caller identified herself as the human-resources representative for the school. She said the vacancy would be filled by a long-term substitute. My heart sank. "But you can apply for that position. All you need to do is complete an online application."

I could do that.

She gave me the access code.

Immediately after hanging up, I went to the computer and brought up the Web page.

I didn't really want to go back to teaching after working at an editing job for the military. However, being an educator was what I knew best. And after being unemployed for more than a hundred days, I knew the bills had to be piling up. Dan had been patient, but I didn't want to live off his income alone forever. He didn't seem to mind, but I struggled with a desire for control and independence.

Sitting at the computer, I scrolled through the job description, clicked on the application link, and filled in all the requested information.

When I got to the dreaded section that asked about any discharges, the whole I-got-fired cycle churned. "Okay, I can do this." I wracked my brain to come up with a concise, legitimate-sounding reason for this professional blight.

"In February 2009," I typed, "I was hired in a new career as a technical editor. I was a federal employee with one-year probation. After six months on the new job, I realized my skill set was different from that required for this particular

work. At the advice of my job mentor, I asked the director of human resources if I could transfer to a position that
involved more collaborative writing assignments. One week
later, I was terminated."

I reread my words and felt proud of myself. That didn't
sound too bad. But then fear crept in. What if I couldn't
even get a substitute-teaching job?

I shook off the doubts and plugged along.

At the end of the long form, I clicked Review. Everything
I'd typed disappeared.

Gritting my teeth, I filled in all the information again.
When I got to the termination explanation, I couldn't
remember the excellent wording I'd come up with previously. I typed what I recalled and filled in the gaps with
new things. Though not as satisfied with the revised version, I clicked Review again. Everything disappeared
again!

After seven times of retyping the same information, all
the insecurities I'd had resurfaced, and I felt stupid to boot.
I couldn't complete one simple online application. What
kind of an idiot can't even fill out a dumb form?

I calmed myself as best I could and called the HR office.

"Hi," I said, "I called a little while ago about an opening.
I'm trying to fill out the online application but am having
some trouble. Is there anyone who could help?"

"I can't help you, but I'll transfer you to Teresa."

The call went to Teresa's voice mail. I left a message.
Then I called the first lady back. "Hi again. You just transferred me to Teresa, but I only got her answering system.
I'm trying to finish this before five o'clock. Can anyone else
help?"

"Oh, I see Teresa. She's over there working on name
badges. I'll transfer you to her office again. Maybe she'll
pick up this time."

I felt my blood pressure rising. Why would the receptionist transfer me when she knew Teresa wasn't by the
phone? I hung up and started slamming keys. I tried three

combinations of buttons to try to get the electronic form to submit. Finally, success!

But I still felt frustrated.

The mail carrier arrived. Hoping there might be some cheery Christmas cards, I hurried outside.

I found one letter from a relative I'd written to recently in an attempt to bridge the gulf that had developed between us. Hoping for a positive response, I ripped open the envelope as soon as I got into the house.

I sank onto the couch as I read my relative's letter. She wrote that she felt betrayed and judged for her divorce six years ago. Her harsh words expressed ongoing pain as well as doubt about my support.

Could this day get any worse?

I had one thing left on my schedule. I'd volunteered to help sort Christmas presents for our church's Angel Tree program.[10] Thanks to this organization, and the generosity of volunteers working in conjunction with them, children with incarcerated parents received gifts on Christmas Day.

Prison ministries started collecting information from inmates in the summer, including the names and ages of their children, so they'd know what presents would be appropriate. The parents would miss hearing the excited shouts of their children opening presents, but at least they'd know the kids had tangible evidence that they cared.

Recalling the faces of several of my favorite students from the prison teaching job, I wondered if they had finished serving their time. Protocol prohibited personal contact. Were any of them involved with the Angel Tree program?

I hoped that by doing something positive and selfless, I could leave behind the day's irritants and find a soothing outlet for my frustrations.

---

10 To find out more about Prison Fellowship's Angel Tree ministry, call 1-800-55-ANGEL or visit www.angeltree.org.

My Cup Overflows

I arrived at the church nursery before my partner, Summer, and found the floor cluttered with mounds of boxes. Deciding to arrange items in a clockwise fashion around the perimeter of the room, I picked up the first present I came to. The tag read, "I love you so much. Daddy."

In the quietness, God whispered the same words to me.

After placing that package along the wall, I picked up another. The tag said, "God has given me a chance to still provide gifts in this time of need. Daddy loves and misses you guys so much."

Humility and gratitude abounded in that father's note. With those few words, he directed his children's attention to a loving God and hope. What more priceless gift could there be?

I reconsidered my own financial worries. How could I be so upset and stressed when others dealt with far worse situations this holiday season?

A box wrapped in blue paper with dancing snowmen had a matching tag with these words: "Merry Christmas, my sweeties. This is our last Christmas apart." The bow, mashed from the stacking, represented the squashed hopes of years spent waiting. Could those dreams be restored?

"Mommy loves you with all her heart," read the tag on a skateboard with a huge golden star in the center.

Beside that sat a cardboard box with a 4T-sized pair of jeans alongside a warm white sweater and small purple snow boots. "I hope I can come home soon to help you with homework and other things."

As I organized the gifts—and absorbed the many expressions of deep emotions—God's presence was strong. In each love note from a parent, I felt as if God were saying the same things to me.

I set a gift-wrapped soccer ball on the padded seat of a rocker, where nursery workers comforted little ones every Sunday. Like those faithful people, I thought, God holds us in his arms and whispers tenderly to us. Sometimes we hear him. Other times we sleep fitfully, but he still watches over us. I imagined him leaning over the crib to tuck me in with soft blankets and then sitting beside me in that chair, rocking until I calmed down enough to fall asleep.

Turning back to my task, I saw an unwrapped card game on the floor. This reminded me of hours spent as a child. I fondly recalled my grandmother teaching me a pastime in which we mixed up cards and dealt them all face down. Players took turns flipping over two of the cards, hoping to find a matching pair. Early in the game, it was hard to figure out where the matches were. But as the rounds went on, and sets of identical cards were removed from the board, it became easier to remember the location of the remaining cards.

I thought life was a bit like this game of concentration, as we try to match our experiences with God's grace. We expect events in our lives to line up in a certain pattern, and we get frustrated when the card's counterpart doesn't immediately appear. Yet if we persevere and pay attention, each new turn in life will reveal more.

Years ago I'd turned up a "divorce" card. That certainly wasn't what I wanted. However, the resulting years of despair over that brokenness had created a gentleness in my spirit that would not have developed otherwise.

The door creaked when the handle turned. "Careful," I warned as Summer peeked into the room. "I've got the door blocked with presents."

I cleared a path and Summer tiptoed around the remaining obstacles. "Sorry I'm late," she said.

"No problem." I knew she had driven forty minutes from her country home in the rain to volunteer while her husband babysat their children.

"Thanks for starting without me."

"I wasn't sure what to do. I put a few in that corner. Is that okay?"

"That's great. I'm just glad you came in to help."

Summer sat cross-legged on the floor and kicked off her shoes, revealing rainbow socks. As I brought her the next package, I couldn't help but notice the pink highlights in her long, black hair and the lip ring that pierced her mouth. She was a bit of a character, but her heart was enormous.

She hummed softly as she worked, her calm spirit permeating the room. When some paper tore as she was wrapping a gift, Summer shrugged and said to herself, "That's okay. I've got more." She looked up at me. "Sorry. I talk to myself sometimes." She giggled, and I joined in, feeling lighthearted for the first time all day.

Together we sorted pages of names, addresses, and gift requests. In what seemed like a very short time, we finished the big job.

"Thanks so much for helping me with this," she said as we cleaned up scraps of wrapping paper, tape, ribbon, and bows.

"I'm glad you let me help," I said. "I've had a horrible attitude all day. This work reminded me that other things are far more important than the frustrations I had to deal with."

She smiled. "Yeah, God often speaks to us in the little things. But it's not always fun listening. Sometimes his correction is hard to take."

I laughed out loud. Her candor refreshed me.

Our next step was to group family packages into large plastic bags. As Summer checked her list, she tilted her head to one side and I noticed a prominent tattoo on her neck.

"Is that a flower?" I asked.

"A tiger lily," she said. "It's not an especially pretty flower. It's actually a common weed. But my dad liked them. They were his favorite. He died when I was twenty."

Summer carried her love for her father so that all could see. I wanted to do the same for my Father.

On the drive home, God kept speaking to me, reminding me of the notes I'd read and of Summer's tattoo. His love provided the antidote to the poisonous doubts I'd allowed to eat away at my spirit earlier in the day.

STUDY SCRIPTURE

How great is the love the Father has lavished on us,
that we should be called children of God!
And that is what we are! (1 John 3:1)

STUDY QUESTIONS

1. Think about a time when you noticed someone giving sacrificially to someone else. What happened? How was your life changed by observing this?

2. Summer's tattoo was a living memorial to honor her father's memory. How does your behavior show respect to your earthly parents and your heavenly Father?

3. What gifts has God given you that you disdain? Why? How might he use that ability to help others?

4. How can you reach out to the broader family of humanity to show love? Think about ministries like the Angel Tree program where you could serve.

5. Imagine the fragrance of sandalwood as a scented oil soaks into your skin. As the perfume drifts to your awareness, the moisture soothes your skin. How can words of hope offer a similar pleasure to others?

CHAPTER ELEVEN

Surely Goodness and Love Will Follow Me

I dressed in a pullover sweater and gray slacks for my job interview. I'd never taught elementary students and felt uncertain that I could adjust to that grade level. My pride barked that I was too "sophisticated" to teach little kids.

But bills were due, and Dan had been carrying all the pressure. After four months of unemployment, I had to get serious about earning some income.

I'd toyed with the idea of becoming an author. The thought greatly appealed to me. But I knew that publishing a book was a long shot, not to mention the unpredictability of royalties in comparison with a regular salary.

My dreams of landing a glorious career hadn't vanished. I still wanted to be someone "important" and shuffle my business cards around as if they represented Park Place on the Monopoly board. However, I was learning—albeit slowly—that God valued heart attitudes more than prestige.

He taught me that fulfillment was about touching lives rather than stroking ego. I'd hit keys on a keyboard for six months in a dark basement before the light dawned on me that I didn't belong in that setting. Even then, the supervisors had to fire me to get me to leave. On occasion, my tenacity was an asset; other times, stubbornness seemed plain stupid.

I wasn't one to stop trying, though. I donned black boots, a long overcoat, and gloves, tucked my portfolio under my arm, and opened the front door. Several inches of snow had fallen overnight, and the houses looked like islands in the middle of a white ocean.

The phone rang inside the house. I checked my watch. Deciding I had a few minutes to spare, I closed the door and hurried to the kitchen.

"I'm so glad I caught you," said Stacie, my friend of twelve years. "Jody had a stroke. An ambulance took her to the hospital yesterday."

I tried to picture Jody lying on a stretcher in the back of an ambulance. That woman never went anywhere without being immaculately attired and coiffed. A slender fifty-nine-year-old, she was the picture of perfect health and exercised regularly.

"She's pretty confused right now and having trouble talking," Stacie said. "I'm on my way to see her right now, and I thought you might want to join me."

"I'd love to, but I have a job interview this morning. I can stop by the hospital after that, though."

After hanging up, I went outside and saw a car stuck in the icy road in front of my neighbor's house, the tires mired in snow. Shane, a forty-year-old who lived alone, had been in a terrible accident a few years ago and spent most of his time in a wheelchair. His ability to talk had also been impaired, and he communicated in grunts that required careful listening and some context for comprehension.

I tiptoed on the ice toward the vehicle and found Shane in the driver's seat, alternating between the gas pedal and the brake, trying to rock the car. His preteen son tried to shovel snow out from under the front right tire while Shane's mom stood beside the car, looking agitated.

"I don't know what we're going to do," she said, her voice trembling. "We're supposed to be at the doctor's office."

"I'll go get another shovel." After dropping my portfolio into my car, I grabbed a shovel from the garage.

Back at the stuck car, I saw the tires spinning. About ten inches of snow blocked the front of the small vehicle. "Maybe we should try to push it," Shane's mom said.

I positioned myself near the left fender, with Shane's petite, sixty-year-old mother on the right fender and his tall, stocky son at the back bumper. I wedged my high-heeled boots into the slippery ground. "Go!" the three of us yelled.

Shane gunned the engine, and the car teetered toward the top of the snow bank. We grunted and pushed harder, only to have the car settle back in the hole.

"Where's your appointment?" I asked, panting.

"At the veterans' clinic on Route One," Shane's mom said.

"I have an interview on the south part of Route One. If you want, you could take my car and drop me off."

"I don't want to be responsible for someone else's car."

"I should be back by noon. Maybe if you called the clinic, you could get a later appointment."

She looked over her shoulder at Shane's steep driveway. "I don't know how I'm going to get him back to the house." Several feet of slick ice lay between the car and the open garage.

I walked to the driver's window, which Shane rolled down. "If your son and I stand on either side of you, are your arms strong enough to hold onto us until we get you to the house?"

Shane nodded and opened the car door. He placed one arm over his son's back and rested the other arm on me. The three of us started toward the house. Shane limped with a halting gait, but his legs held up.

We'd covered about four steps when the boy groaned and slumped under his dad's weight. *Shane must be leaning harder on his son to spare me.* We still had about eight feet to go. But we couldn't turn back.

"C'mon," I rallied. "We can do this." I looked at Shane's mom, who hovered nearby. "Get the wheelchair."

She pulled the chair out of the garage and wheeled it to the bottom of the driveway. Shane grabbed the back of the chair and collapsed onto the seat. I pushed him the last couple of slippery steps until the wheels leveled on the garage floor. Shane's mom looked back in frustration at her stranded car.

I didn't want to leave, but I was going to be late for my interview.

As I crossed the cul-de-sac, Ethan came out of his house and waved at me. The teenager had helped me many times when Dan was gone. He'd repaired a weed eater, mowed the yard, and even removed a snake from the yard for me.

"Oh, Ethan, I'm so glad you're here. Can you help me back out of my driveway and then work on Shane's car?"

"Of course." Ethan directed me as I inched the car out of the driveway. As I drove down our street, I saw Ethan through the rearview mirror, helping Shane's son shovel snow near the back tire.

A pothole in the packed ice jarred me. I navigated the snowy roads, trying to drive carefully in spite of being late for my appointment.

Once on the main road, my tires faithfully gripped the surface and I sped up a bit. With one minute to spare, I pulled into the entrance and parked.

A perky lady greeted me inside. "How may I help you?"

"I have a ten o'clock job interview."

She smiled. "The interviewer isn't here yet, but you can have a seat over there and wait for her."

Grateful that I wasn't later than the person I was supposed to meet, I sat and flipped through my portfolio, which included letters of recommendation and samples of creative writing done by students at the prison. Memories of special people and events flooded through my mind. I realized how many people had touched my life and enriched it over the years. These connections were the most valuable assets I carried forward.

The receptionist caught my eye. "Would you mind watching the door for a minute while I run to the bathroom?"

"Sure."

She had barely left when the phone rang. She ran back to answer it. "Yes, the applicant's here." The receptionist held her hand over the receiver. "She can't get her car out of the driveway. Would you mind waiting a little longer?"

I thought about Jody. The road from the school board office to the hospital would surely be plowed. Deciding my time could be better spent with my friend, I asked if I could leave my portfolio and have the interviewer call me if she was still interested in seeing me.

I left the office feeling disappointed, but I refused to get discouraged. The results were in God's hands. If he wanted me to work at that elementary school, he could make it happen.

At the hospital's information desk, I asked for Jody's room number. Before the elderly volunteer could look it up, a male voice answered, "I believe you'll find her in 2021." I looked up and saw a Catholic priest wearing a black robe, plaid scarf, and beret.

"I'm Father Riley," he said with a lilting brogue. "I was just up there. She has several people with her." Knowing Jody's priest was on the job comforted me.

I thanked him and headed to Jody's room. She sat in a chair, looking as fragile as a porcelain doll. Her ash blonde hair was uncombed; her normally sharp blue eyes were dull and gray. Wires were hooked to her chest, and cords ran down her teal tunic and slacks. Jody's son and daughter-in-law perched on the small bench across from her.

Stacie stood near the doorway, her black hair and dark eyes contrasting with the antiseptic white room. "I just saw Jody's father," I whispered.

An odd expression crossed Stacie's face. "Her father?"

"I mean the priest."

Stacie breathed a sigh of relief. "Good. Her dad died years ago."

Stacie's son, Jamie, made room for me on the seat closest to Jody. I sat down and lightly patted her arm. "How are you doing?"

Her lips worked hard to make words. "Not a . . . hundred percent." Her optimism shone through, even in these circumstances, but anxiety hovered in the room.

"Does that mean you haven't organized the entire hospital wing?" I quipped.

Jody smiled, and some of the tension in the room lifted.

"How did your interview go?" Stacie asked me.

Before I could answer, Jody exclaimed, "You got an interview?"

I told Jody about the potential teaching job. Behind me, I heard Stacie whispering to Jody's son, Joe.

When I finished, Jody turned her attention over my shoulder. "What are you two talking about back there?"

Stacie took Jody's hand. "I was telling Joe how wonderful it is that you remembered Tracy didn't have a job. Yesterday you didn't know anyone's names."

"And every time a new doctor came in," Joe added, "he asked the same questions and each time you gave a different answer."

Jody looked scared.

"But today you got my joke about organizing the hospital right away," I said. "So there's obviously nothing wrong with your ability to think."

Jody relaxed a bit. "It's hard finding . . . " The pause lasted uncomfortably long as she struggled to talk.

". . . the right words," I finished for her.

She nodded.

"You must have an injury to the part of your brain that processes speech."

A handsome middle-aged man with broad shoulders burst into the room. "I was at church this morning for prayer time, and someone said we should pray for Jody. I wanted to see how you are."

With six people now packed in the tiny room, all surrounding Jody with love and concern, I decided to leave. "I love you and I'll see you soon," I said to Jody, vacating my seat for the new visitor.

I left the hospital thinking about how this woman's life mattered because she had showered goodness on people in many ways. *I want to be like that.*

The roads still were a mess, so I drove slowly. My windshield kept getting splashed with mud from the traffic. The wipers didn't spray water, so I couldn't clean off the spots. I stopped at Little Tire on the way home to see if the mechanics could unclog the washer-fluid line.

"Hi. I don't have an appointment. But my wipers aren't working. Would you have time to help?"

The short man nodded. "Are the blades moving?"

"Yes. It's the squirter thingy that's the problem."

He smiled at my vast technical knowledge. "I'll take a look."

Less than ten minutes later, he pushed the keys across the counter. "All I had to do was reconnect the wire."

I pulled out my wallet, wondering whether I'd have to write a check or put this on my credit card. "How much do I owe you?"

"Five bucks."

Relieved, I handed him a bill. "Thank you so much."

My morning had gone extraordinarily well as so many people had demonstrated admirable qualities of compassion and kindness.

When I pulled into the driveway, I saw that the postal service had left a small box on the front step. The return address was my dad's. I took the package into the house, opened it, and found a wooden bowl with a small plaque that read, "Give us this day our daily bread." The accompanying note said:

> Darling girl,
> Another year has passed and it's time to assess our blessings. You are a special blessing that inspires me to look beyond the obvious and to aspire to be a better person. You have handled difficulty and adversity in your life and still maintain a good heart. I'm glad you have taken some time off to "smell the roses." Know that I will always love you.
> Poppy
> P.S. Thanks for allowing me to share my blessings with you and Dan.

Wrapped within this precious note was a generous check.

I sat on a chair and sobbed. The tenderness in the note and the abundant gift touched a deep place in my soul. Dad and I had experienced plenty of conflict—and we'd probably would disagree many more times, since we were both strong willed. However, he loved me, and these thoughtful gifts and words expressed that.

I savored that moment of feeling wrapped in love. If the day had ended right there, nothing could have made it better. But more gifts poured in.

In the mailbox that afternoon, I received a small red package containing a pair of silver earrings from my sister and a card from my mom that read on the front, "How do you gift wrap perfect love?" When I opened the card, it played a song about God's indescribable love. The inside of the card pictured Jesus in the manger.

Mom had written a note in her elegant, curly script:

You are most special, and from day one, a treasured gift from God. I love you. Mom

She also had included a check as a gift for the Christmas holiday. As I was dabbing my eyes with a napkin, the phone rang.

"Hi, Mom," said my older son, calling from college. "I'm coming home for a visit. I'll be there in three hours." I hadn't seen him in weeks.

"Be careful driving," I cautioned. "The roads here haven't been plowed."

He chuckled. "I'm always careful, Mom."

"I can't wait to see you."

As I sank onto the kitchen stool, I noticed the small print at the bottom of Mom's card. It said, "Enjoy the miracle."

There had been many that day—and I was certainly enjoying them.

SCRIPTURE

…make every effort to add to your faith goodness; and to goodness, knowledge; and to knowledge, self-control; and to self-control, perseverance; and to perseverance, godliness; and to godliness, brotherly kindness; and to brotherly kindness, love. (2 Peter 1:5–7)

STUDY QUESTIONS

1. Evaluate the progression of the attributes mentioned in the Scripture passage quoted from 2 Peter. Discuss with your small group or a friend why you think the list begins with faith.

2. Think about a time when you exercised self-control. How did that experience help develop perseverance?

3. How would you distinguish "brotherly kindness" from "love"? Cite examples.

4. Who is a modern celebrity demonstrating goodness?

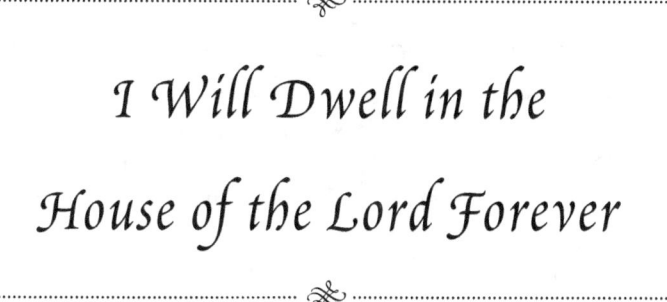

CHAPTER TWELVE

I Will Dwell in the
House of the Lord Forever

The new year began with Ohio State facing Oregon at the Rose Bowl. Dan watched the game preview from our couch. I sat beside him, observing the four captains of each team walk onto the field, holding hands. That gesture of unity in burly adult men touched me. Those professional athletes practiced teamwork, a skill I'd worked hard to acquire.

After feeling betrayed at my editing job, the climb from the pit of aloneness had been steep, but God had not abandoned me. He stood beside me in the turmoil and sent many people into my path to help. From Dan, I learned unconditional love. From our kids and friends, I rediscovered nonjudgmental acceptance. From acquaintances, the delightful surprises of "God connections" never ceased to amaze me. I might have bumps and bruises from playing on the field of life, but with God as my coach, I didn't have to worry.

On the television, the referee displayed a coin, then the grand marshal threw it. Oregon won the toss, but the captain deferred the choice to the Buckeyes.

"Why'd he do that?" I asked Dan.

"It's a psychological thing," he said.

"You mean they're showing the opposing team they can handle whatever they dish out?"

"Yeah."

A captain had to have tremendous assurance in his team to make such a decision. That same certainty came with faith in God. I didn't need to have all the answers or possess all the talent in the world. I just had to trust him to lead and be obedient when he did. Demonstrating faith during adversity glorifies our Father and shows the strength of our defense to the opposing team.

God certainly had protected us. Dan didn't get fired. His supervisors rallied around him, and the new product received positive reviews from an outside source. I still wasn't sure about my own employment, but I knew God wanted me to keep writing. After decades of dreaming about authoring a book, I finally had a topic to write about. Who would have thought that being fired would be the beginning of a new life for me?

John, the Human Resources director who effected my termination, transferred to another agency soon after. Before leaving, he e-mailed Dan about an educator position available on base. "Tell Tracy she can use my name as a reference if she wants to try for the job."

Dan didn't respond. A week later John came by his office and asked where Dan got his suits tailored.

"Why in the world did he do that?" I asked.

"I don't know," Dan said. "I guess he knew he hadn't done right by you and that was his way of making up."

Even though John facilitated my firing, God used that job loss to deepen my faith. The Lord had not failed to provide for me.

As my human eyes strained to see beyond my circumstances, several Bible stories came to mind that gave me hope.

In one Old Testament account, Joseph's jealous brothers sold him into slavery. His boss's lustful wife lied about him. Unfairly sentenced, he was forgotten for years in prison, yet still Joseph served faithfully. Once he was released, God favored him with the job of administering food throughout the nation during a severe famine.

When Joseph reconciled with his brothers years later, he told them, "You intended to harm me, but God intended it for good to accomplish what is now being done, the saving of many lives" (Genesis 50:20).

Television announcers interrupted my musings as they discussed which team was favored to win. Three of the four selected Oregon State, one wearing the Duck mascot on his head and quacking. The last man reluctantly supported the Buckeyes. Broadcasters showed game clips from the 2009 season. Both teams had rebounded from slow starts and obstacles to qualify for this bowl.

Do difficulties forge us into something stronger than we would be otherwise?

How would I finish this season of my life? I wanted to make a comeback. But my Coach had called a time out. I wanted to charge back onto the field for victory. But I needed to let him call the plays. I wouldn't argue. *Well, at least not much.*

The other players on my team were doing well but also struggling. Jody, for example, was recuperating from her stroke at home. She had no memory of her days in the hospital, and speaking still presented challenges. Her son and daughter-in-law, who had provided round-the-clock care for two weeks, planned to go back to their house soon. Jody would be alone again with many unknowns.

She called and asked me to pick up her Christmas present for me since she couldn't drive.

"I can swing by your house at lunch tomorrow. Do you need anything?"

"I'm getting low on . . ." She paused. "Hold on. I'll find the word."

"Bread or milk?" I offered.

"No." She paused again. "Green beans. For the dog."

I could have guessed a lot of things, but vegetables for her dog wouldn't have been one of them. "You got it. I'll see you tomorrow."

I reminded myself that every tomorrow held opportunities for another miracle. I often lost sight of that outlook in the chaos of everyday life and the disappointment of unexpected moments like being fired.

Jody hadn't anticipated having an aneurism, but she bravely faced her challenges, which included short-term memory loss and relearning how to talk. Despite her stilted speech and carefully chosen words, I heard determination in her voice.

Tammy, my friend with health and family issues, experienced relief from her adrenal-gland problem. Her son Arnold got a job and had settled into an apartment. However, another concern popped up when doctors discovered Tammy had a tumor that required surgery.

Letha, a friend from church, called to ask if I would take over leading a women's Bible study on Sunday nights since the regular teacher couldn't continue. This wasn't the teaching opportunity I had anticipated, and no pay was involved. But this group of ladies had supported me, loved me, and ministered to me during the devastating years after my divorce. I felt honored to be invited to give back.

At the urging of the Holy Spirit, I phoned a woman I hadn't talked to in many months and asked if she'd like to attend.

"I really could use a Bible study to see what God can do with my life now," she said. "Did you know I just spent two and a half months in jail?"

"No! I had no idea."

"The charges came from my problem with alcoholism."

"We all have our areas of difficulty," I said, not wanting her to feel embarrassed about sharing her struggles with me. "Did I tell you I got fired this summer?"

"No," she said, sounding surprised.

"I haven't found a new job. I'm also still working through post-divorce issues with my boys. So I know what it feels like to be broken. I'm here for you. I love you."

"I love you too," she responded quietly.

I didn't have that kind of unconditional love a few years ago. I was so full of my own "righteousness," I would have judged someone who struggled with alcoholism as weak. But circumstances had humbled me and softened my heart. I wanted to embrace people in pain the way God and others had held me in my despair.

An Old Testament story in Ezekiel tells about invaders endangering the Israelites. But God protected his people and defeated the vast foreign army. "Then those who live in the towns of Israel will go out and use the weapons (of the defeated enemy) for fuel and burn them up—the small and large shields, the bows and arrows, the war clubs and spears. For seven years they will use them for fuel. They will not need to gather wood from the fields or cut it from the forests because they will use the weapons for fuel" (Ezekiel 39:9–10, parentheses added).

God converted wooden instruments designed for destruction into household resources. The captured weaponry from the invading forces provided the town with firewood for seven years! I pictured the Israelites' outlook changing from terror to delight at their deliverance and the abundant supply that fell at their feet.

God does the same kind of miracle today. He transforms damaging events into embers that ignite hearts with compassion and wisdom.

When I considered my life "perfect," I couldn't reach out to others, but sorrow had equipped me to share hope.

Painful experiences—marital estrangement, divorce, and job termination—fueled growth that would have been impossible otherwise. Before those incidents, the only knowledge I had about overcoming was in my head, not my heart.

A few days after my conversation with the woman battling alcoholism, I visited a local meeting of Alcoholics Anonymous to learn how people shared their strength and hope with one another.

Men and women, young and old, sat in a circle. Some had yellowish complexions, dull eyes, and sunken cheeks. Their hands shook as they clutched paper cups of black coffee. A few faces shone with confidence birthed from freedom and life beyond the enslavement to substances. The people with years of sobriety—emotional and physical—kept coming back, testifying that there was a path to healing. They issued a clarion call to newcomers that recovery could bring peace and restoration.

That night's discussion centered on relating to one's higher power.

One man in his forties struggled out loud with the mighty question: "Why?" He couldn't understand how a loving God could allow suffering in the world. "At my work, many young people are walking in the same hell of addiction that I'm climbing out of. Why do they have to go through that? If I can recover, why can't they?"

The room fell into a pregnant silence, until another man said, "God doesn't cause pain. But he does allow us free will."

Another man added, "I learned a lot from the consequences I suffered. That's what helped me change."

I waited to see if anyone else would speak. When no one did, I said, "Some of our deepest hurts become our greatest opportunities. In my twenties, I was raped. Fifteen years later, God used that experience to enable me to reach out to one of my high school students who had the same thing happen to her."

I surprised myself by revealing such intimate information. That wound from my past was rarely mentioned. But I wanted to honor the question about where God was when life seemed to fall apart.

"In my forties, I got divorced," I continued, hoping that sharing my experiences would be beneficial to the people around me. "God used that devastation to develop in me a compassion for those facing marital problems that I wouldn't have had otherwise."

Several people looked me in the eye, their expressions communicating strong interest in my words. Some stared at the floor, trying to process the message as it applied to their own circumstances.

"Last summer I got fired. That certainly wasn't fun. But in the past few months, God has shown me new goals and helped me figure out how to work toward accomplishing them. In my quiet time recently, I asked God why he hadn't blessed me in my editing job. In my heart, I heard God say, 'I did bless you! I got you out of there.'"

The group laughed.

"I don't have all the answers about suffering. I don't think anyone ever will. However, if we choose to look beyond our brokenness, our pain can be redeemed by helping others."

Following the meeting, I approached the man who had cried. "I know what you mean about wondering why bad things happen. I've done a lot of that too. Would you like to know something that has helped me?"

"Sure."

I wrote on a piece of scrap paper, "Ask, and you shall be answered. Seek and you shall find. Knock, and the door shall be opened unto you. Matthew 7:7."

He took the note and read it. "Thanks."

"That was the first Bible verse I ever memorized," I said. "It comforts me to know that I can ask God anything and he will provide the answer."

Sorrow's burden diminishes with fellowship. That was true in the AA meeting, and I found it proven in my friendships as well.

My neighborhood Bible study group planned an outing to a tea shop in downtown Fredericksburg. On the Saturday morning we were supposed to meet, Shellie called.

"I can't go today because my son's buying a car. He doesn't know how to drive a stick shift, so I have to go with him."

Selfishly, I wanted Shellie to join us. Her quiet strength resonated in soft-spoken wisdom and genuine interest in others. But I respected her priorities. After all, she worked full time and had several children. "I understand," I said. "You need to take care of your family."

"Thanks," she said, sounding relieved.

After we hung up, I thought about what an encouragement Shellie had been to me the past few months. We'd met at church ten years ago. Then she moved out of state for a while, and I lost track of her. Three months before I was fired, we ran into each other at the grocery store. And on the day I got fired, she'd called me out of the blue. God had renewed our connection in a season when we needed each other.

I drove to Alison's house to pick her up for the tea outing. Alison was another trusted confidante with whom I had shared many doubts and joys. I wanted to tell her about Shellie. But as soon as she got in the car, she said, "I have some news. My dad died Thursday."

I reached over the center console and hugged her. "Why didn't you call me?"

"I did, but there was no answer. I didn't want to leave a message like that. Besides, I knew I would see you today."

I felt awful that I hadn't been available when Alison needed me. She'd made the one-hour trip to see her dad for weeks, grieving each time she saw him as she watched his health and mind deteriorate. But all that preparation still couldn't have made the end easy. "Were you with him at the time?"

"No, he went during the night. The nurses found him on Friday morning and called my mom." She dabbed her eyes. "When I saw him Thursday morning, he was so weak he couldn't hold up his head. I didn't understand why God would let him linger like that."

"Are you sure you feel like going out today?"

She smiled. "Oh, yes. I've been looking forward to this. It'll be good to think about something else."

I put the car into gear and drove in silence for a while, praying that God would give me the right words to say to comfort my friend in her grief.

Alison said, "I'm glad we had the going-home party for Dad. At least he got to see all his friends one last time."

"It's great that he was able to visit with everyone and enjoy the company. Remember how he sneaked off in the cab to see his old office too?"

Alison surprised me with a deep belly laugh. We grinned, remembering her dad's escapade leaving the hotel party without telling anyone so he could go by his former work place. I was glad Alison fondly remembered her father. He had been quite a character. I hoped I could be as loving and steadfast a daughter for my dad when his time came.

"I took several of his personal items home," Alison said. "And I put up more of his pictures around the house."

I think God does that too. He has rows and rows of photographs of his children proudly displayed on the mantel in his home. Some highlight our innocent, childlike days, playing hide-and-seek with him. Other images record our rebellious youth when we encountered difficult choices and tasted temptation. I believe the pictures he treasures most are those of our maturity, with faces lined from times of suffering when we chose to turn our eyes toward him.

God gazes fondly at the family album as he waits for us to come home. When he sees us approaching, his arms will open wide in an embrace that will last forever.

STUDY SCRIPTURE

Do not let your hearts be troubled. Trust in God; trust also in me.
In my Father's house are many rooms; if it were not so, I would have told you.
I am going there to prepare a place for you.
And if I go and prepare a place for you,
I will come back and take you to be with me…
(John 14:1–3)

STUDY QUESTIONS

1. Describe how hearing someone else's testimony has encouraged your faith walk.

2. Identify two people with whom you can develop a closer relationship. Name three specific steps you can initiate to deepen those fellowships.

3. Invite someone you respect to meet with you on a regular basis to pray. What area of growth do you want to highlight in those meetings?

4. Set your watch, then sit for five full minutes in quiet. How can rest and reflection change your outlook about time and how you want to invest it? Write three areas for change you want to prioritize.

5. Can you recite from memory Psalm 23? If not, look it up again on the page before the table of contents. Use the space below to rewrite it in your own words. Remember that God is always with you, no matter how difficult circumstances may seem at the time.

www.ingramcontent.com/pod-product-compliance
Lightning Source LLC
Chambersburg PA
CBHW070136290526
45789CB00002B/504